UNAUTHORIZED
AMERICA

Also by Vince Staten:
REAL BARBECUE (with Greg Johnson)

UNAUTHORIZED AMERICA

AMERICA

—

A TRAVEL GUIDE
TO THE PLACES
THE CHAMBER OF COMMERCE
WON'T TELL YOU ABOUT

VINCE STATEN

PERENNIAL LIBRARY

HARPER & ROW, PUBLISHERS, NEW YORK
Grand Rapids, Philadelphia, St. Louis, San Francisco
London, Singapore, Sydney, Tokyo, Toronto

FIRST EDITION

Designer: Ruth Kolbert

Library of Congress Cataloging-in-Publication Data

Staten, Vince, 1947–
Unauthorized America: a travel guide to the places the chamber of
commerce won't tell you about/Vince Staten.—1st ed.
p. cm.
ISBN 0-06-096514-2
1. United States—Description and travel—1981——Guidebooks—
Humor. I. Title.
E158.S78 1990
917.304'928—dc20   89–46119

91 92 93 94 DT/RRD 10 9 8 7 6 5 4 3

For Will and Judy

CONTENTS

Acknowledgments

It's impossible to pinpoint the exact genesis of this book. I can trace my fascination with unauthorized tourist sights to 1970 when a carload of college friends and I drove to Fayetteville, North Carolina, to try to get a look at the *Fatal Vision* murder site. We were on our way to the beach and it seemed like an interesting side trip.

And over the years I have accumulated an amazing collection of postcards of questionable taste: a Before and After view of the Florida Skyway bridge, which collapsed after a freighter crashed into the southbound span, plunging several cars and a bus into the murk and killing thirty-four; an Assassin's Lair postcard from the Texas Book Depository in Dallas; a postcard of Hank Williams Sr.'s death car . . . let's stop the list here.

The idea began taking shape while I was researching my last book, *Real Barbecue*. I traveled 25,000 miles and sampled 400 barbecue joints. After visiting these strange, wonderful barbecue joints I discovered that normal tourist attractions bored me. There was no excitement to seeing historical markers and ancient battlefields. Not after visiting a barbecue joint where the owner slept next to his pit while cooking because, as he put it, "a man that won't sleep with his meat don't care about his barbecue." Not after visiting a barbecue joint where the owner was rude to all the customers . . . and they loved it. Not after visiting a barbecue joint with a wall painting of Jesus' family tree tracing his lineage all the way back to Adam and Eve.

I got in the habit of asking the locals to direct me to any interesting sights that weren't in the travel brochures. And invariably they sent me to celebrity death sites and UFO landing locations. "That's where Charles Manson grew up," one told me. And that spot is in this book.

David McGinty, editor of the (Louisville) *Courier-Journal Sunday Magazine,* helped refine the idea to an unauthorized travel guide.

Kris Dahl, who is as much an editor as she is an agent, put on the finishing touches.

Maureen Brown, my research assistant, was able to track down some locations that I had given up on.

Chris Wohlwend, a longtime accomplice, was my Atlanta tour guide.

Moral and immoral support came from my *Real Barbecue* co-author, Greg Johnson.

True-crime-book fans Pat and George DeChurch contributed significantly to the Best-selling Murder Sites chapter.

John Thorne suggested Whitaker Chambers's pumpkin patch.

Matt Mirapaul thought of the Unlikely Events chapter and made invaluable clippings contributions.

John Shelton Reed told me about the atomic bomb that hit South Carolina.

Bob Moody told me about Jerry Lee Lewis trying to bump off his little sister. He also helped with the Baltimore sights.

Others who contributed along the way were Gary Burbank, Pat McDonogh, Elizabeth Owen, Jim Reed, Bill Bramlette, Anne McCoy, J. B. Brown, Ed McClanahan, Bob Hill, Ronni Lundy, Alana Nash, Ellie Brecher, C. Ray Hall, Chip Nold, David Inman, Jena Monahan, Arlene Jacobson, Warren Payne, Sally Nichols, Leslie Ellis, Martha Elson, Dick Kaukas, Sarah Fritchner, Cindy Inskeep, Elmer Hall, Diane Heilenmann, Jane Fleischaker, Marty Bass, Anne Kellan, Maureen McNerney, Karen Smith, Sherri Arnett, and Carol Burch.

Mary Caldwell sent the Florida Skyway postcard.

And, of course, thanks to my editors at Harper & Row, Hugh Van Dusen and Stephanie Gunning.

WELCOME TO WALLY WORLD

When Rick London would escort friends and relatives from his native Hattiesburg, Mississippi, around his adopted hometown of Washington, D.C., he noticed a peculiar effect the sights of the nation's capital had on them.

"I'd take them to the Capitol or the White House and you could see their pupils dilating and then they would glaze over. They had seen this stuff on TV so often and studied about it in school, it just had no effect on them. They were immune to awe. Then after a while, one or the other of them would whisper to me, 'Where's Gary Hart's town house?' and I'd take them. That's what they really wanted to see. The stuff they'd been reading about in the paper."

And thus was born Washington's Scandal Tours, which served more than 100,000 tourists in its first year.

No monuments or statues for these tourists. They get the real thing:

- The Tidal Basin where a drunken Wilbur Mills saw both his career and his companion, stripper Fanne Foxe, sink beneath the waters.

1

- The spot on the Capitol steps where John and Rita Jenrette enjoyed a different kind of congress.
- The congressional cloakroom where, the tour guide says, a homosexual congressman "let his fingers do the walking through the House and Senate pages."

Scandal Tours is solving the problem many modern vacationers face: many of the best spots aren't in the travel guides.

If you follow the brochures, you'll see John F. Kennedy's birthplace, but you won't see Lee Harvey Oswald's boardinghouse room, complete with Oswald artifacts. That's because for years the St. Augustine (Florida) Chamber of Commerce refused to include the Tragedy in U.S. History Museum, with its reproduction of Oswald's room, in tourist guides or allow it to place brochures in the local tourist center.

The travel brochures never mention JFK's Love Nest, where he and Marilyn Monroe would meet for an afternoon tryst, or Elvis's Drugstore, where the King loaded up on downers.

But let's face it: not everyone wants to spend summer vacation watching Junior slither down the water slide or trailing Grandpa as he treks from one historic marker to the next.

Not everyone wants a Disney World vacation.

This book boldly dares to take you where no travel brochures have taken you before, to the out-of-the-way sights and the offbeat vacation spots nobody touts.

This is an underground guide to America, to the places that you *Really* want to see: where John Lennon was shot, where Margaret Mitchell was run over by a car, where Sean Penn punched out a photographer, where Fawn Hall shredded boss Ollie North's papers.

These are the places the local Chamber of Commerce won't tell you about. But we will.

Get the motor warming, Mildred. You're in for a vacation like you've never had before.

Now put it in Drive and go!

RULES OF THE GAME

Because these sights are unofficial and our tour is unauthorized, you can't just put on your Hawaiian shirt and barge in. There are rules:

Rule No. 1: Don't disturb the current owners of any of the homes on our tour. If you've ever bought a house, you know you're lucky to find out if the garage leaks, much less if a former resident was Charles Manson.

Rule No. 2: If it says "call ahead to make an appointment," it means "call ahead to make an appointment." You don't like it if your mother-in-law just drops in, do you?

Rule No. 3: If you can't find it, ask. Don't be afraid to stop and ask for directions. That's what I did. Most folks are more than happy to guide you. They are just like you and me: they're more interested in the scandalous than the safe. When I was in Biloxi, Mississippi, searching for Jayne Mansfield's death site, the folks there went out of their way to help me, and out of their way to tell me that Miss Mansfield hadn't just been killed, she'd been decapitated.

Rule No. 4: Don't bother celebrities. Actress Pam Dawber has launched a campaign to prevent ordinary folks from rummaging through California's Department of Motor Vehicles Bureau records to find celebrity addresses. She has a good reason. That's how the deranged assassin who killed actress Rebecca Schaeffer located the actress's apartment.

That's why there are no current celebrity addresses in this book. And a couple of others are a little vague: the 1200 block of Whatever Avenue.

There are directions to almost every site in the book. If there are no directions, it means you are better off using a map.

There are no directions to New York City places because no one drives—or should—in Manhattan.

A few sights are so remote and the roads so unremarkable that you have to ask for directions from a local. Like Blanche DuBois, I had to count on the kindness of strangers for sites and directions.

Memories fade. I've double-checked everything I

could against published sources and official records, but there still may be an error. If you know about one, let me know. And let me know about sights you'd like to see in a future edition: the sights you show people in your town and ones you'd like to see. Write me at Box 293, Prospect, KY 40059.

HISTORIC BATTLE SITES

O nce upon a time vacation meant packing the kids in the car and visiting a national monument or driving by the site of some historic battle.

But the modern tourist family isn't interested in Old Geezer geyser or Musty monument.

For the modern tourist a historic battle site is the place where Sean Penn decked a photographer. And a national park is where JFK parked and made out with Marilyn Monroe.

This chapter takes you to those famous fight sites.

THE NEW SULTAN OF SWAT:
THE SEAN PENN SCUFFLE TOUR

Sean Penn has to be America's most underpaid middle-weight. The sour-faced actor has gone at least six rounds with various photographers, friends, and wives and received nothing in return. Except for publicity.

Here is a self-guided tour of Sean Penn Fight Sites:

- In Nashville in 1985 to film *At Close Range*, he became enraged at a photographer trying to take his picture from close range, heaved a rock at him, then camera-whipped him for the insolence demonstrated by continuing to take pictures. Penalty: $100 fine and a ninety-day suspended sentence.

- At a nightclub in L.A.'s Silver Lake area on April 12, 1986, with his boy-toy Madonna, he became enraged when one of her old friends, songwriter David Wolinski, pecked her good night on the cheek. He began pummeling the man with his fists, then kicked him and threw a chair at him. Charge: Misdemeanor battery. Penalty: $1,700 fine and one-year probation.

- On the set of the movie *Colors* in April 1987, Penn became enraged when he spotted an extra, Jeffrey Klein, taking his picture. He approached the man, spat on him, and became even more enraged when the extra spat back. He punched the extra with his fists and had to be pulled off him by crew members. The sight of the extra further enraged Penn, and he had to be restrained three times by crew members. Later that same month he was stopped on suspicion of drunken driving. He had just run a red light. He failed a field sobriety test. Total charges: reckless driving, battery, violating probation. Total penalty: probation revoked. Sentenced to sixty days in jail. Served thirty-two days at the Mono, California, county jail.

- In August 1987, as Penn returned from filming in West Germany to begin his jail stint, he shoved television cameraman Bob Tur who was trying to photograph him at Los Angeles International Airport. Charges: none filed. Penalty: bad publicity. Rude remarks about his violent temper and "other problems."

- In June 1988 at the Mike Tyson–Michael Spinks fight at Trump Plaza in Atlantic City, Penn fought a preliminary bout with a cameraman from a Philadelphia TV station. Cameraman Al Pollock claimed Penn kicked him in the leg. Penalty: more bad publicity, continuation of immature image.

- On the Upper West Side of Manhattan he kicked a dent in the car of a photographer who was following him and Madonna.

☆ Getting There:
- In Nashville the incident occurred in front of the Clarion Maxwell House hotel, 2025 Metro Center Blvd. From I-65 south, take I-265. The hotel will be right off Exit 1.
- The nightclub incident was at Helena's at Lafayette Park Place and Temple St. in L.A.'s Silver Lake area. From the Hollywood Freeway (US 101), take the Alvarado St. exit south one block to Temple. Go west on Temple eight blocks.
- The *Colors* set was at Ocean Front Walk in Venice, California. Just look for the roller skaters and the skateboarders. That's where it happened.
- He was pulled over for suspicion of drunken driving at the corner of Fairfax Ave. and Washington Blvd. in Los Angeles.
- He shoved a television cameraman at Los Angeles International Airport. It happened near the elevators to the parking lot.
- He shoved another television cameraman at Trump Plaza in Atlantic City. It's on the Boardwalk at Mississippi Ave.
- He kicked the photographer's car at 65 Central Park West on the Upper West Side of Manhattan, in front of the apartment building where he and Madonna lived.

THE MARTIN CHRONICLES

The late Billy Martin proved he was a better battler than batter in 1957 when he and New York Yankee teammates Mickey Mantle, Whitey Ford, and Hank Bauer were involved in a celebrated brawl at New York's Copacabana Club.

Martin never met a man he didn't like well enough to punch.

Let's follow Martin's Greatest Hits:

- In 1969 Martin, then the Minnesota Twins manager, punched out his best pitcher, Dave Boswell, in a fight outside a Detroit bar.
- In 1978 Martin punched out a Reno sportswriter during an interview. (Journalists, take heed!)
- In 1979 Martin fought an Illinois marshmallow salesman, Joseph Cooper, in a Bloomington, Minnesota, hotel.
- In 1985 Martin, then Yankees manager, suffered a broken arm during a fight in a Baltimore hotel bar with his own pitcher Ed Whitson. The fight began in the bar, continued in the lobby of the hotel, and ended in the parking lot.
- On May 7, 1988, Martin brawled with three men in the restroom of an Arlington, Texas, topless bar. Martin was hospitalized overnight for observation.

☆ Getting There:
- The Copacabana is at 10 East 60th St. in New York City. Sammy Davis, Jr., was being heckled by guys in town for a bowling tournament when words were exchanged between the bowlers and the Yankees.
- Martin punched out pitcher Dave Boswell outside the Lindell AC bar at 1310 Cass Ave. in Detroit. It's still open. From the Detroit courthouse go down Michigan Ave. and take a right on Cass.
- He punched out the sportswriter in the bar of the Centennial Coliseum in Reno.
- He slugged marshmallow salesman Cooper just outside the bar of Chez Colette at L'Hotel de France in Bloomington, Minnesota. It was at 5601 West 78th St. It's now the Sofitel. There is a thirty-foot-long hall between the bar and the hotel lobby. The fight occurred at the archway, about halfway down the hall.

The Copacabana: Billy Martin fight sight.

- Martin brawled with pitcher Whitson at the Cross Key Inn Lounge at 5100 Falls Rd. in Baltimore.
- Martin fought with three men in the restroom of Lace, a topless bar at 2711 Majesty Dr., one mile from Arlington Stadium in Arlington, Texas. The street is between I-30 and State Highway 360. It's best to use a map.

GEORGE STEINBRENNER VERSUS ELEVATOR

It was Los Angles and you know how those Los Angelinos can be: they were insulting New York Yankees owner George Steinbrenner, ragging him about the poor performance his team was making against the hometown Dodgers in the 1981 World Series. George took matters into his own hands and slugged the two gents, breaking his hand and busting his lip in the process.

At least that's the way George tells it.

Most everyone else assumes hothead Steinbrenner took a punch at the elevator in frustration over his team's performance—the Yanks had just lost their third game in a row to the Dodgers—seriously injuring himself in the process. Rather than take the ribbing for his self-inflicted injury, he apparently invented the elevator fight story. The gents he supposedly punched out have never been seen or heard from.

☆ **Getting There:** It happened on the way to the tenth floor of the Hyatt Wilshire at 3515 Wilshire Blvd. in Los Angeles. From the Santa Monica Freeway (I-10) take Western Ave. to Wilshire and turn right.

KENNETH, WHAT IS THE FREQUENCY?

On October 6, 1986, New Yorkers woke up to one of the most bizarre stories the city had seen in some time—this in a city that sees a lot of bizarre stories.

It seemed that the previous evening CBS News's big bucks anchorman Dan Rather had been mugged by a well-dressed attacker whose only statement to Rather was "Kenneth, what is the frequency?" Rather fled to a nearby apartment building. The attacker and a well-dressed accomplice followed and beat him to a pulp, all the while asking, "Kenneth, what is the frequency?"

No one has yet figured out what the frequency was.

☆ **Getting There:** Rather was attacked on Park Ave., near the 1075 Building, where he fled to escape the attackers. Tell the cabbie to take you to 1075 Park Ave. on the Upper East Side.

LET'S ALL GO TO THE LOBBY

Clarence M. Dees had gone to one of those multi-screen theaters, North Park Cinemas in Lexington, Kentucky. He purchased a ticket to one movie, got bored with it, and moved to another theater to check out that picture. When he tried to return to see the end of the original picture, he was stopped by employees. Words were exchanged and he was asked to leave.

But he didn't go straight home. Fifteen minutes later he returned, in his tractor-trailer, crashing into the lobby, tearing out the ceiling, and tipping over the video games. He narrowly missed demolishing the ticket and concession stands. Police Sergeant Fred Williamson said Dees told him he wanted "to put it in there far enough to see the movie he paid to watch." Dees was charged with wanton endangerment and criminal mischief.

☆ **Getting There:** North Park Cinemas is at 500 New Circle Rd. NW in Lexington. From I-64-75 you can take any of the Lexington exits west. They run into New Circle Road.

HIS WAY OR TAKE THIS #*$

During the forties Hearst newspapers columnist Lee Mortimer was merciless in his attacks on Frank Sinatra. He called him the "4-F from Hasborough Heights" and charged him with cowardice for his abbreviated overseas tour entertaining troops, noting that Frankie had waited until late in the war to make his first overseas journey.

On the evening of April 8, 1947, Sinatra got his long-awaited revenge. According to Kitty Kelley's unauthorized Sinatra bio, *His Way,* when Mortimer and his date were leaving Ciro's nightclub Sinatra and four goons trailed him to the door, where Sinatra sucker-punched him. Mortimer fell and the goons held him down while Sinatra continued to pummel him.

Mortimer swore out a warrant charging assault and battery and also filed a civil suit seeking $25,000 in damages. He received two anonymous threats of violence if he didn't drop the charges. He ended up settling out of court for $9,000.

☆ **Getting There:** Ciro's was also the site of another Historic Battle, this one between Johnny "Tarzan" Weismuller and his wife, the Mexican Spitfire, Lupe Velez. That one ended with John dumping his dessert in Lupe's lap. Now in West Hollywood is the Comedy Store. Take Sunset Blvd. west from the Hollywood Freeway. It's at 8433 Sunset Blvd.

SAN FRANCISCO BATHS

If you measure a person's success by the number of column inches written about him in newspapers, then talk show host Morton Downey, Jr., was at the top of his field. Unfortunately for Downey, television executives measure success by advertising dollars. And by the spring of 1989, advertising on Downey's controversial talk show was down, way down.

Then, as if sent by a PR agent from heaven, came the report by Downey that he had been attacked in the San Francisco airport bathroom by a band of Nazi skinheads who had crayoned swastikas on his face. His grafitti-ed face was plastered on front pages across the country.

Then airport spokesman Ron Wilson said there were no signs of a fight in the restroom. Others came forward expressing doubts about the veracity of Downey's claim because the swastikas were backward, as if penned by looking in a mirror. It was the last straw and his loud-mouthed show was canceled.

☆ **Getting There:** It's the men's room on the second level right by the United Airlines ticket counter.

REDD VERSUS THE DUKE

They were two of the biggest celebrities in Hollywood at the time, the time being the summer of 1973. John Wayne was The Duke, star of hundreds of cowboy pictures. Redd Foxx was Fred Sanford, the crotchety trashman on the TV hit "Sanford and Son."

They had just taped a summer special for NBC and were gathered in the side parking lot, along with Glenn

Ford, Porter Wagoner, Dolly Parton, Dan Rowan, Dick Martin, Howard Cosell, Kent McCord, Harry Belafonte, Bob Newhart, Ernest Borgnine, and Ed Asner.

Let's let Jim Reed, who was the security guard in the lot, pick up the story. "After the taping was over, they herded everybody outside and proceeded to stage their arrivals. The crowd on hand in actuality was there to watch the 'Tonight Show.' They had rented searchlights simply for the fake arrival. And they had to tape it after the show because they had to wait 'til dark. Everything was fake but the fight."

The fight began because some thoughtless person had assigned John Wayne and Redd Foxx to ride in the same limo.

"Wayne would have none of it. And Redd was upset, yelling at him, calling him a redneck. It kind of reminded me of a fight at a ball game because Redd came up to about Wayne's belt buckle. Then they started pushing each other. Somebody called 'Guard!' which happened to be me. I had to step in between and push them apart. If John Wayne had decided to do otherwise, I would have taken my hat off on the spot and given up my security job. I wasn't about to tangle with him. He was a big guy."

Reed, who is six feet tall and sturdily built, managed to wedge himself between the potential pugilists and saved the day. And the night.

☆ **Getting There:** The Carson show and other NBC specials were taped then, as now, at NBC's Burbank, California, studios. The address is 3000 West Alameda, Burbank. From the Ventura Freeway take Olive Ave. north to Alameda. Go right and it's right there.

The fight occurred in the news parking lot. If you are on Alameda facing the entrance, it is to the right, the little parking lot. Reed says, "It's not normally a good spot to star gaze. They usually take the stars around back to the main parking lot."

INQUIRING MINDS WANT
TO GO

—

A dmit it. When you first read about Bess Myerson's arrest on shoplifting charges, the first thing you asked wasn't, Why, oh, why did she do that? It was, What did she steal and where did she steal it? And when you heard that it was $44 worth of nail polish and cheap earrings from a discount store, you wanted to hop in your car and go see the store.

Let's see, right here is where she must have stuffed the nail polish in her bag, and over there, that's where she filched the ear bobs and tucked them in her coat pocket. And by the way, Mr. Manager, where was her car, the one she said she had to lock up before going back into the store to pay for that stuff?

Right, Bess, it happens to all of us.

Let's hop in the car and hit some Great Scandal Sights.

—

THE BESS MESS

There she was, Bess Myerson, Miss America of 1945, hauled in front of a judge and charged with conspiracy, mail fraud, bribery, and attempting to obstruct justice. All because she allegedly tried to help her rich boyfriend get his alimony payments reduced.

What did she do that was so wrong? Well, for starters she allegedly tried to bribe a judge by giving the judge's emotionally troubled daughter a job in city government. Then after the judge reduced her rich boyfriend's alimony payments and investigators started sniffing around, she supposedly told the judge's daughter to "keep your big mouth shut."

Her "rich boyfriend" was Carl "Andy" Capasso, a millionaire sewer contractor whom she met in 1980 when she was running for the Democratic nomination to the Senate. (She lost.)

She was fifty-six; he was thirty-five. She was single and available; he was married with five kids and a reported net worth of $12 million. It was love at first sight, and soon she was wheeling around town in a $41,000 midnight blue Mercedes. Then came all that Bess Mess. But in December of 1988 a jury of her peers, if there is such a thing, acquitted her of all the charges.

Still, what came out in court was quite a mess.

If you want to follow the trial of the Bess Mess, start in Westhampton Beach at 37 Exchange Place. This is the Capasso home that Bess shared with Andy beginning in January 1983, just after he filed for divorce.

☆ **Getting There:** Take the Sunrise Highway on Long Island to Old Riverhead south. It runs into Westhampton Beach.

Next head into Manhattan to 900 Fifth Ave. This is the location of Andy's luxury condo, which was at the heart of the divorce settlement. Judge Hortense Gabel, perhaps inspired by Bess's generosity in putting daughter Sukhreet Gabel on the public teat in 1983, slashed Nancy's alimony payments from $1,850 a week to $680 after Sukhreet's good fortune in the job market.

For more on Bess's little shoplifting problem, see Sticky Fingers, page 32.

THE WAGES OF SIN...

... Are actually pretty good when you look at what happened to some of the crowd caught in the Gary Hart–Donna Rice scandal.

Lynn Armandt, Rice's one-time close friend, pocketed $125,000 for a revealing interview with *People* magazine and another $25,000 for the photos of Hart and Rice she provided to the *National Enquirer*.

Donna Rice did a photo layout for *Life* for $4,000, signed as spokeswoman for No Excuses jeans, and received a $100,000 advance from ABC, which wanted to produce a two-hour TV movie called *The Donna Rice Story*. Rice and ABC later parted in a disagreement over the direction the movie should take.

All for behavior that would have been passed off as the lifestyles of the young and the restless were it not for the fact that one participant, Gary Hart, was old and a presidential candidate.

Think about that: if it weren't for Donna Rice, Gary Hart might be President today. And what a horrifying thought that is.

Rumors of what the media like to call "womanizing" had surrounded Hart for years. But the rumors didn't break into the open until April 1987 when the *Miami Herald* splashed a story across its front page about its investigative stakeout on Hart's Capitol Hill home. The investigative team had spotted Hart and a young woman, not his wife, entering on Saturday but not leaving until Sunday.

Soon all America knew about "model and actress" Donna Rice. She even did a Barbara Walters's special. That's how America rewards scandalous behavior.

If you want to see the sites where Gary Hart's libido outpaced his presidential aspirations, check out these places:

The story actually begins before the incident in Washington. It begins on the *Monkey Business*, a yacht that Gary and Donna co-navigated to Bimini. The yacht is currently at the Turnberry Yacht and Country Club in Florida. About that trip, Donna would later tell a news conference:

"I was invited [by Hart] to go on the boat for a trip . . . . I didn't quite know where. . . . I invited a girlfriend of mine [Lynn Armandt] along. We set out and ended up in Bimini. . . . We walked around the town, came back to the boat, getting ready to leave, and obviously customs had closed. . . . We were stuck. We had planned on turning right back around. It was not like we set sail for somewhere down in God knows where. So anyway, we were stuck there and decided to cook out and we came back the next morning. . . . The two men slept on Bill's [Broadhurst] boat, and Lynn and I slept on the boat we came over on. Even though there were plenty of cabins on that boat we had come over on, I guess we felt for appearance sake

Gary Hart's townhouse.

that was . . . proper." Broadhurst was a member of Hart's campaign team.

Lynn would later contradict Donna's story in the *People* magazine cover story.

☆ **Getting There:** The *Monkey Business* is currently docked at the Turnberry Yacht and Country Club, where you can rent it for $2,500 a day, according to Captain Vogelsang. That includes use of the boat's Jacuzzi and luxury bar. The eighty-two-foot boat is owned by Turnberry Club owner Don Soffer. It's at 19735 Turnberry Way. The phone number is (305) 932-6200.

Gary Hart's old town house—he no longer owns it—is at 517 Sixth St. SE on Capitol Hill. The *Miami Herald* staked out the place after receiving an anonymous tip from a female caller who identified herself as a liberal Democrat. She told the *Herald* Hart was "having an affair with a friend of mine" and "we don't need another President who lies." From the rear of the Capitol go east to Fourth St. Go south on Fourth to G St. Go east to Sixth and north on Sixth (you pretty much have to take this route because Sixth is one way north).

FAWN HALL'S SHREDDING ROOM

The flaxen hair, the gleaming teeth, the to-the-point answers—Fawn Hall was everything the loyal secretary is supposed to be. And she could type. But her duties went beyond answering the phone and buying the missus a Christmas present. She shredded government property, destroyed evidence, and smuggled documents out of the Executive Office Building, all at the behest of her beleaguered boss, Lieutenant Colonel Oliver North. "I believed in Colonel North. . . . I did as I was told," she told the Congressional committee investigating the Iran-Contra affair. She was so loyal she even turned down a jeans ad, a *Penthouse* proposition, and a movie-of-the-week offer. Give this woman a medal.

Fawn Hall's shredding room.

☆ **Getting There:** Fawn and Ollie destroyed incriminating documents in his office, Room 392 of the old Executive Office Building. It's the five-story rococo building at Seventeenth and Pennsylvania Ave. NW, next to the White House.

JIMMY THE GEEK'S RESTAURANT

It was Martin Luther King's birthday, and convicted-but-pardoned felon Jimmy the Greek Snyder was eating dinner with friends at Duke Zeibart's in Washington, D.C. When a local TV reporter approached the famous CBS oddsmaker and asked if he would go on camera to make a few comments about the progress of black athletes and administrators in sports, the Greek answered Sure.

What followed was a conversation that ended the Greek's long, if not celebrated, career in TV sports.

Among other things Jimmy the Geek said:

- Blacks were "bred to be the better athletes because this goes all the way to the Civil War when, during the slave trading, the slave owner would breed his big woman so that he would have a big black kid."
- "If they [blacks] take over coaching like everybody wants them to, there's not going to be anything left for white people."

The Geek explained his comments to the *Washington Post:* "I was laughing and kidding when I said those things. I was joking."

Pretty funny stuff, huh? CBS didn't think so. They canned him within hours.

☆ **Getting There:** Duke Zeibart's restaurant is at 1050 Connecticut Ave. NW in Washington, D.C. From Pennsylvania Ave., take a left onto K St. Take K St. to Eighteenth St. and make a right. Park in the second lot on the right-hand side of that street, in the middle of the block (Washington Square Parking). Get a ticket and go up the elevator to the Terrace Level, where the restaurant will validate your parking ticket.

SCHOOL FOR SCANDAL

The McMartin Pre-School in Manhattan Beach, California, burst into the national conscience in 1984 when "20/20" revealed that the school's seven teachers, including founder Virginia McMartin, were being charged with child abuse and molesting children by playing such games as Naked Movie Star.

But four years later, after a new county attorney reviewed the case, only two of the seven were tried.

Raymond Buckey, then twenty-eight, was charged with eighty counts of child molestation and one count of conspiracy. His mother, Peggy McMartin Buckey, then sixty, daughter of the school's founder, faced twenty counts of child molestation and one count of conspiracy. Their trial became the longest, most expensive trial in U.S. history. Peggy was acquitted of all charges. Ray was acquitted of most. He faces retrial on thirteen charges.

☆ **Getting There:** The McMartin School is at 931 Manhattan Beach Blvd. in Manhattan Beach, California. From the San Diego Freeway (I-405) take Inglewood Ave. south to Manhattan Beach Blvd. Go west. Weeds have grown up but there is still school yard equipment around.

FATTY, FATTY, TWO BY FOUR

The pudgy actor had risen from an extra in the Keystone Kops comedies to star and had just signed a $3-million three-year contract with Paramount. To celebrate, Fatty Arbuckle transported five hundred friends and business

Scandal site: McMartin Pre-School.

associates to San Francisco for a party over the Labor Day weekend of 1921.

During the drunken revelry Arbuckle dragged a tipsy starlet named Virginia Rappe into a bedroom, ripped off her clothing, and raped her, perhaps with a Coke or champagne bottle.

She died from injuries sustained in the assault, and although Arbuckle was acquitted of all charges, his movie career was over.

☆ **Getting There:** The party was in Suite 1221 in San Francisco's Hotel St. Francis. It's now the Westin St. Francis and it's at 335 Powell St. at Union Square. From the Golden Gate Bridge, take the Marina District exit. You'll be on Lombard St., in the right direction. Take a right on Van Ness, a left on Post, a right on Powell, and then a right on Geary—which will take you into the hotel's garage. For reservations call (800) 228-3000.

S.P.A.Z.Z.

The support group S.P.A.Z.Z. was hastily created in the summer of 1989 to rally national support for the beleaguered celebrity Zsa Zsa Gabor. Zsa, the more quotable of the famed Gabor sisters, was in hot water again. After Beverly Hills cop Paul Kramer stopped her because her Rolls-Royce's license plate was expired, he discovered the same thing had happened to her driver's license. Not only that, but there was an open container of alcohol in her convertible.

When the officer took what seemed an eternity (anything over two minutes is an eternity to a Gabor sister) to run her ID through R&I, Zsa Zsa climbed back in her car and raced off. The policeman overtook her two blocks down the road and told her she was under arrest. Naturally she slapped him, and the next thing she knew it was spread eagle, Miranda, the whole nine yards.

She claimed she had renewed her plates but there was a bureaucratic snafu. She also claimed the flask of bourbon in the glove compartment belonged to her husband, Prince Frederick von Anhalt the Eighth (eighth husband, that is). Zsa did admit, "Sometimes I use it to sweeten my Diet Pepsi."

She wasn't charged with altering her driver's license, although authorities did note that someone (not Zsa Zsa, said Zsa Zsa) had scratched out the birth date 6/6/23 and penciled in 2/6/28. And lowered the weight.

Oh, S.P.A.Z.Z. stands for Society for the Prevention of Anything Against Zsa Zsa. It was founded in Orlando, Florida, by president Paul Spreadbury.

☆ **Getting There:** Zsa Zsa was stopped on LaCienega Blvd. But the real tourist site, the one you'll want to go to, is the corner of Olympic Blvd. and Le Doux Rd., where she slapped "that gorgeous officer." From the Santa Monica Freeway (I-10) take LaCienega Blvd. north and west on Olympic one block to Le Doux Rd.

Earlier in 1989 she had been removed from a Delta flight for loosing her Shih Tzu dogs in the first-class cabin of the aircraft. She was put off at the Delta terminal at Atlanta's Hartsfield Airport. If you fly anywhere in the southern United States, you've changed planes in Atlanta. It was in the Delta pod that Zsa was booted.

HEARTS AND FLOWERS

It was not the sort of behavior you expect from a virtuoso violinist, but on July 26, 1989, police arrested Eugene Fodor at the Vineyard Harbor Motel in Martha's Vineyard on drug and weapons charges. Hotel maids discovered the violinist sleeping in a room listed as unoccupied. He reportedly tried to pay for his night's stay, then bolted from the lobby, raced to the room, and locked the door. Police were called; drugs were found; charges were filed.

Police said Fodor had twenty grams of cocaine, a small amount of heroin, a dagger, a hypodermic needle, and some pills. He was held overnight in jail after the Edgartown district judge refused to accept his three-hundred-year-old violin to guarantee bail.

☆ **Getting There:** Vineyard Harbor Motel is on Beach Rd. in Martha's Vineyard. Coming in off Vineyard Harbor, take a left where the ferry boat lets you off. Follow the harbor. The motel is one block down.

HAIR ON FIRE

You've probably heard the expression before: "I'd rather run down the street naked with my hair on fire." Comedian Richard Pryor took it seriously on June 9, 1980, when he accidentally caught his hair, and shirt and pants, on fire while free-basing cocaine. He really did run down the street with his hair on fire, and as he later noted in a comedy routine, "When you run down the street with your hair on fire, people will get out of the way."

☆ **Getting There:** Pryor ran down Hayvenhurst Ave. in the San Fernando Valley. He ran the two blocks south from Parthenia St. to the aptly named Chase St. From the Simi Valley–San Fernando Valley Freeway (SR 118) take Hayvenhurst south about twenty-four blocks to Parthenia. Then get out and run the next two blocks.

SAY IT AIN'T SO, PETE

Peter Edward Rose, as the court documents called him, is baseball's all-time hit leader and the holder of numerous other career longevity records. During his three decades in organized baseball, he had earned an enormous amount of money. He had also made an enormous amount of money selling memorabilia and autographs. But he wagered an enormous amount on football and other games (but not baseball, of course). The late baseball commissioner A. Bartlett Giamatti banned him from baseball for life for his transgressions. At a press conference, Rose denied betting on baseball but accepted his lifetime ban as "fair." That same night he showed up on the Cable Value Network, selling baseball bats and plaques.

At this writing he is under investigation for evading income taxes.

☆ **Getting There:** One of Pete Rose's bookies was identified in newspaper accounts as Ron Peters, owner of Jonathan's Cafe in Franklin, Ohio. It is at 202 South Main St. in Franklin, Ohio. From I-75 take Exit 38 west to Route 73. Jonathan's is at the corner of Second St. and Route 73.

The Cable Value Network is at different points on the dial on various cable systems.

I SLEPT WITH A TRUMPET

That *New York Post* headline said it all. The story was about the sensational Pulitzer divorce trial that included insinuations that Roxanne Pulitzer might have performed unusual, even difficult, acts with a trumpet. Roxanne denied it. Vehemently. She admitted she owned a four-foot aluminum trumpet and that she kept it in the bedroom. But she was not, she cried, a strumpet with a trumpet.

☆ **Getting There:** The trumpet was kept in the bedroom of the Pulitzers' Palm Beach, Florida, home at 410 North Lake Way. Take the North Lake Blvd. exit from I-95.

WHERE JESSICA HAHN LOST HER VIRGINITY

Depends on who you talk to.

Jessica said in *Playboy* it was the Sheraton Sand Key Hotel in Clearwater Beach, Florida, where evangelist Jim Bakker forced himself on her.

But former madam Roxanne Dacus claimed Hahn worked for her at a Long Island bordello in 1977–78, long before Hahn's tryst with Bakker. Dacus first made the charge in *Penthouse* magazine, then told a news conference, "You can't be a prostitute for as long as she was and not be experienced." Dacus said the then-eighteen-year-old Hahn handled "up to forty men a night." She described Hahn as aloof. "She had the attitude that she was better than the other girls. She had the attitude that she was the madam and I was working for her."

Hahn, of course, denied the accusation.

Penthouse publisher Bob Guccione, of course, said his magazine stood by the story.

(Possibility No. 3: Hahn later testified in an Albany, New York, courtroom that she had an affair with Long Island preacher Gene Profeta before and after her sexual encounter with PTL founder Jim Bakker.)

We're not picking sides. We're just telling how to get to the most famous possible sites.

☆ **Location No. 1, Getting There:** Jessica said in *Playboy* it was in Room 538 of the Sheraton Sand Key Hotel in Clearwater Beach, Florida. You can stay there for $138 a night. Clearwater Beach is in the Tampa–St. Petersburg area. The Sheraton is at 1160 Gulf Blvd. From US 19 Alternate take SR 60 to Clearwater Beach.

☆ **Location No. 2, Getting There:** Roxanne Dacus's whorehouse was at 318 North Hickory Rd. in North Massapequa, Long Island. Take the Southern State Parkway on Long Island. Take Exit 29, Hicksville Rd., north into town. It is no longer a whorehouse.

PICKRICK PICK HANDLES

Lester Maddox was a small-time restauranteur until that fateful day in 1964 when he refused to serve three black divinity students who had wandered in, wanting nothing more than a fried chicken dinner.

Maddox later stood at the door of his restaurant, the Pickrick, with an ax handle, threatening to club any blacks who tried to enter. His scrappiness appealed to Georgians, who elected him governor in 1967. His most famous accomplishment as governor was riding a bicycle backward. Today he is a real estate salesman.

The Pickrick is no longer a restaurant. Maddox sold it to Georgia Tech, and the school converted it into the Fred W. Ajax Student Placement Center.

☆ **Getting There:** The old Pickrick is at 891 Hemphill Ave. on the campus of Georgia Tech.

SERVING MANKIND, PART ONE

When Alferd Packer stumbled into Ute, Colorado, in the spring of 1874 after being trapped in the Rockies all winter, living, by his own account, off pine gum, rosebuds, and his own moccasins (roasted), the locals set up a table in his honor and loaded it down with goodies. Alferd passed, asking only for a shot of whiskey.

Soon folks were asking questions like, Why isn't Alferd eating? And Doesn't Alferd look a little pudgy? And What happened to those other five fellows who went prospecting with him?

Alferd told several versions of his story over the next ten years but never once did he deny what he ate during that cold winter: his fellow prospectors. He was eventually convicted of killing his friends and eating them, his main crime being that he diminished the Democrats of the county by five. He served fourteen years in prison before spending his last years as a security guard at the *Denver Post*. He died in 1907.

☆ **Getting There:** The massacre site is in Lake City, Colorado, and is marked by a plaque. If you make it to Lake City, just ask. There are only 231 year-round residents and anyone can direct you.

The cafeteria at the University of Colorado in Boulder is named in Packer's honor, and each year students celebrate the end of school with a rib-eating contest.

SERVING MANKIND, PART TWO

It was the wild, wild west and a caravan of covered wagons was crossing the Sierra Mountains when a blizzard suddenly blew in from the north, trapping the wagon train at the pass. Things were fine for a few days but then rations began running short.

That's when George Donner cut his hand on a chisel. Gangrene set in, George died, and some hungry pioneer yelled, "Soup's on."

The Donner Party is celebrated at the Donner Party Museum in Truckee, California. You can even see the chisel that George cut his hand on.

☆ **Getting There:** The museum is two miles west of Truckee. From Highway 80 take the Donner State Park exit to 12593 Donner Pass Rd. For information call (916) 587-3841.

THE GHOST OF SUZY PRESENT

To her bosses at the *New York Post* she is Aileen Mehle.

But to the rest of the world she is Suzy, people columnist supreme, confidante of the stars, scourge of upstart gossipists, friend of flacks.

If Suzy says something, you can take it as gospel. At least you could. Until the fateful day during the summer of 1988 when her rival, an upstart gossip columnist at the competing *Newsday* newspaper, revealed that Suzy wrote about a party at the Metropolitan Museum of Art, meticulously describing the guests and the banquet table, when in fact Suzy was nowhere near the gala she described and, in fact, several of the guests she "spotted" had been unable to attend.

In short, columnist James Revson had blown the whistle on Suzy, revealing that she wrote portions of her column from —gasp!—press releases.

Suzy 'fessed up, admitting she wasn't there. "I am just

back this minute from a little vacation on the beautiful, windswept isle of Mustique in the Caribbean. It was heaven." She apologized, saying she "should have yanked the whole thing or at least the names the [press] release said would attend." Still, she demonstrated a bit of moxie in adding, "I bow in accuracy and meticulousness to no one." And before her readers could swallow that swollen-headed remark, she launched into an attack on Revson, calling him a "rat," a "liar," and a "snake." And for good measure she ended with a little warning to New York's publicity-conscious hostesses: she wouldn't attend any event to which Revson was invited—"Just call it a boycott —or even a Suzycott."

As pseudojournalists are wont, Suzy got in the last word: "I'm Mount Rushmore, just as majestic. They will be left squirming on the ground."

☆ **Getting There:** You can be where Suzy said she was, but really wasn't, the Metropolitan Museum of Art. It's at Fifth Ave. and Eighty-second St.

THE ORIGINAL "GATE"

Who put the "gate" in all the "gate" scandals (Korea-gate, Iran-gate, Etc.-gate)? Watergate, that's who. Watergate was the original "gate" scandal. And really the best.

It was in the early morning hours of June 17, 1972, that five suspects were found hiding in the Watergate offices of the Democratic National Committee. Before this "third-rate burglary" was solved, it had brought down the President of the United States, Richard M. Nixon.

☆ **Getting There:** The Watergate Building (it's also a hotel and apartment complex) is at 2650 Virginia Ave. in Washington, D.C. The Democratic headquarters were on the sixth floor.

E. Howard Hunt and G. Gordon Liddy were in Room 214 of the Watergate Hotel, monitoring the break-in with

Watergate scandal sites: The Watergate office building and Howard Johnson's.

walkie-talkies. They were in the room of burglars Bernard Barker and Eugenio Martinez. Burglars Frank Sturgis and Virgilio Gonzalez had checked into Room 314. Ex-FBI agent Alfred Baldwin was across the street in Room 419 of the Howard Johnson Motor Inn, watching the proceedings through binoculars.

THE WIT IN THE WRINGER

The most famous quote to come out of the Watergate affair (after Nixon's "I am not a crook," of course) was former Attorney General John Mitchell's colorful description of what might happen to those in journalism who went after the administration. When *Washington Post* reporter Carl Bernstein told Mitchell that the newspaper was running a story saying Mitchell had controlled a secret reelection committee slush fund, Mitchell replied, "[*Post* publisher] Katie Graham's gonna get her tit caught in a big fat wringer if that's published."

☆ **Getting There:** The Mitchells were living in Room 710 (Marriott Suite) in New York's Essex House on Central Park South when Bernstein called.

CHUCK BERRY AND THE MANN

Rock and roll pioneer Chuck Berry had met a cute lady at a cantina in Juarez, Mexico, and invited her back to El Paso to watch his show. She followed along on the tour and wound up back in St. Louis, working as a hostess at Berry's nightclub. Then on December 21, 1959, Berry was arrested for violating the Mann Act, which made it illegal to transport a female across state lines for immoral purposes.

A month later he was indicted for a second violation, this time for a trip he had made eighteen months earlier, taking a St. Louis woman along with him to Topeka, Kansas.

☆ **Getting There:** Berry was charged with bringing the first woman to work at his club, Chuck Berry's Club Bandstand in St. Louis, at 4221 West Easton Ave., which is now Martin Luther King Blvd. The second violation was a result of an arrest at the Interstate 70 viaduct in St. Charles, Missouri. It's Exit 228.

STICKY FINGERS

I f you are poor and unknown and steal a doughnut to feed your starving little boy, you get six months in the clink. If you are rich and famous, everyone knows how valuable your time is and you can walk away from the deli counter with a bagel without paying and claim you were too busy to be waiting for that fool of a clerk. And you get off.

OOPS! FORGOT TO LOCK MY CAR

In May 1988 former Miss America Bess Myerson—who was already in hot water over favors she did to help her boyfriend (like allegedly bribe a judge)—was picked up for attempting to shoplift six bottles of nail polish, five pairs of earrings, a pair of shoes, and flashlight batteries, $44 worth of merchandise in all. Bess claimed she planned to go back in the store to pay for the items after she locked her car.

☆ **Getting There:** The Hills department store, part of a discount chain, is at 560 Montgomery Pike South in South Williamsport, Pennsylvania. From Lewisburg, take Route 15 just about all the way to Williamsport. Hills will be on Route 15 just before you get to Williamsport.

Bess was in the area to visit her boyfriend Andy Capasso, who was then residing at nearby Allenwood prison, serving a four-year sentence on a tax-evasion conviction. See Celebrity Hard Time, page 187, for more on that.

HAND TOOLS ARE EASY, BUT TRY STUFFING A TWENTY-POUND BAG OF DOG FOOD IN YOUR SHORTS

Former Cleveland Mayor Carl Stokes, the first black mayor of a major city, was charged in July 1989 with stealing a twenty-pound bag of dog food worth $17.25 from a pet shop in a suburb of Cleveland. He was acquitted by a jury after he claimed he couldn't get waited on. But it wasn't his first problem with sticky fingers. Months earlier he admitted stealing a $2.39 screwdriver from a hardware store. He paid the store $50 in restitution and charges were dropped.

☆ **Getting There:** The dog food incident occurred at Pad and Fin Pet Store, 16719 Chagrin Blvd. in Shaker Heights, Ohio. From I-77 south, take Highway 480 east to Highway 271 north. Make a left at the Chagrin Boulevard exit, and make a right at Lee Street. The pet store is a quarter of a block east of Lee on the corner of Chagrin and Lee. (Enter the New City Bank parking lot and go around to the back; you'll see a sign for the pet store.)

The hardware store was the Handy Andy Home Improvement Center at 436 Northfield Road in Bedford, Ohio. From I-77 south, take Highway 480 east to the Warrensville-Northfield exit. Make a right at the light; the store is four miles down on the right side at the corner of Northfield and Rockside.

JOHN JENRETTE

ABSCAM Congressman John Jenrette, who had already served some time for that little escapade, was arrested in 1989 for stealing a pair of shoes and a tie from a department store in suburban Washington and altering prices on a pair of pants and a shirt. Jenrette called the whole thing a mistake. He claimed he was trying on the rubber work boots when he left the store to check whether his car was being towed. Does he know Bess Myerson?

In 1989 a Fairfax County (Virginia) Circuit Court jury found him guilty of petty larceny. "I have great remorse," he said at the time of sentencing.

☆ **Getting There:** It happened at the Marshall's Department Store at 8353 Leesburg Pike in Vienna, Virginia. From I-95 north, take I-495 north to Frederick. Exit 10-B at Tyson's Corner; the store is one mile ahead on the left.

SHOP 'TIL YOU PICK SOMETHING UP

Margo Adams, Wade Boggs's angry ex-girlfriend, was accused of shoplifting a $258 coat from Nordstrom, a department store in Costa Mesa, California, in March 1989. For more on Margo see Dangerous Liaisons, page 77.

☆ **Getting There:** The Nordstrom is at 3333 Bristol St. in Costa Mesa, right off Highway 405 at Bristol.

ECSTASY AND ME

In 1966 retired actress Hedy Lamarr, star of such films as *Algiers* and *Ecstasy,* was charged with stealing $86 worth of clothing from the May Company in Beverly Hills. She beat the rap.

☆ **Getting There:** The May Company is at 6067 Wilshire Blvd. From the Santa Monica Freeway (I-10) take Crenshaw north to Wilshire and go left on Wilshire.

MIKE TYSON'S FIGHTS

—

Jack Dempsey had Gene Tunney. Floyd Patterson had Ingemar Johansson. Muhammad Ali had Joe Frazier. Favorite opponents.

But Mike Tyson hasn't had a favorite opponent. He's taken on all comers: man, beast, woman, tree, parked car.

ROUND ONE:
VERSUS A PARKED CAR

On May 8, 1988, heavyweight boxing champion Mike Tyson and his wife of three months, Robin Givens, were driving on Varick Street in downtown Manhattan when his silver Bentley went out of control and hit a parked car. Two Port Authority cops arrived and Tyson gave them the keys to the $185,000 car. According to Jose Torres's book *Fire & Fear,* Tyson was distracted because he and Robin had been arguing over condoms she found in his pocket. He swerved to avoid hitting a cat. Instead he hit a parked car and two guys who were standing near it. He gave one

35

guy $500 and the guy immediately ran to the Off Track Betting parlor across the street. After he gave the cops his Bentley, they shooed off the other guy.

☆ **Getting There:** It was in Greenwich Village at Varick and Spring near the entrance to the Holland Tunnel.

———

ROUND TWO:
VERSUS MITCH GREEN

In the early morning hours of August 23, 1988, heavy-weight boxing champion Mike Tyson ran into his old friend Mitch "Blood" Green outside what has been re-ferred to in the media as an "all-night men's apparel store." One thing led to another, and before long the two men were conversing the only way they knew how, with their fists. It was a split decision: Tyson split his finger and Green split his head.

Still it was a better outcome for Green than their pre-vious match in 1986, when Tyson outpointed Green in a unanimous decision.

Let's back up here. Mike Tyson was where at four-thirty in the morning, an all-night men's apparel store? Right.

He was there, he told the media, to pick up a custom-made, white leather jacket that was inscribed: "Don't Be-lieve the Hype."

He had to pick it up at four-thirty in the morning?

Tyson claimed Green attacked him. Green, for his part, accused Tyson of sucker-punching him.

☆ **Getting There:** Dapper Dan's Boutique is at 41 East 125th St. in Harlem. Phone is (212) 289-8896. Take a cab. Re-quest the driver to wait out front.

ROUND THREE:
VERSUS A TREE

During Labor Day Weekend 1988 Tyson ran his BMW into a tree on Camille Ewald's property in Catskill. (Camille was the companion of his late manager Cus D'Amato and a mother figure to Tyson.) He was taken to Greene County hospital in Catskill, then Hudson Memorial Hospital before wife Robin Givens insisted he be taken by ambulance to Columbia Presbyterian Hospital in Manhattan, where he registered under the name Cisco Esteban. His injuries were diagnosed as minor but enough to postpone his upcoming fight with Frank Bruno.

Tabloid reporters said it was a suicide attempt.

No one else believes he tried to kill himself in a car with an air bag.

☆ **Getting There:** The Ewald property is at Thorpe Rd. and Route 385 in the town of Athens, New York. Coming off the New York State Thruway, take a left. Go down to the bypass. Go east toward the Rip Van Winkle Bridge. Take a left at the traffic light (where Route 385 intersects). Go north for two and a half miles until you get to Thorpe Rd. The property will be on the right-hand side, across the street from a small, square telephone building.

ROUND FOUR:
VERSUS HIS MANSION FURNITURE

On Oct. 2, 1988, Bernardsville, New Jersey, police were summoned to Tyson's $4-million, twenty-eight-room estate to investigate reports of violence. Tyson had hurled furniture out the windows and flung a fireplace and-iron through a foyer window in a fit of anger over statements wife Robin had made to Barbara Walters the previous Friday night on "20/20." What? Telling Barbara and a national television audience that her marriage to Mike was "torture . . . sheer hell"?

No one was hurt and no charges were filed. "It's his

home. He's entitled to do anything he pleases, providing no one is injured," a police officer said. Wife Robin was reported to be in Los Angeles at the time.

☆ **Getting There:** The mansion is Kenilworth and it's on fourteen acres on Ravine Lake Rd. in Bernardsville, New Jersey.

ROUND FIVE:
VERSUS A PARKING LOT ATTENDANT

Tyson was at the Greek Theater in Los Angeles to see the rap group Run-DMC when he had his next fight. Theater worker Tabita Gonzalez said she was in the parking lot when Tyson asked her for a hug. She thought he was a bodyguard for the band and agreed. He thought it was an invitation for more. Jonathan Casares, parking lot supervisor, arrived to see if she was all right. Tyson threw a T-shirt at him and shoved him back inside his golf cart with a stiff arm to the face, hard enough to cut Casares's lip. Also hard enough for a lawsuit, of course. Casares eventually got seventy-five grand for his cut lip, Gonzalez thirty grand for her pinched butt or whatever.

☆ **Getting There:** The Greek Theater is at 2700 North Vermont Ave. From the Hollywood Freeway take Vermont Ave. north. It's in Griffith Park.

ROUND SIX:
VERSUS A DISCO HABITUÉ

Sandra Moore claimed in a lawsuit that on December 10, 1988, Tyson "violently and forcibly" grabbed her, "forcibly fondling her and embracing her against her will." She said $4.5 million would suffice as recompense.

☆ **Getting There:** The incident, if you want to call it that, occurred at Bentley's at 25 East 40th St. on Manhattan's East Side.

Bentley's: where Mike Tyson fought.

ROUND SEVEN:
VERSUS ROBIN GIVENS

The celebrity and TV actress married Tyson after telling him she was pregnant with his baby. Then she told him she miscarried but since they were already married, what the hey. Then she told Barbara Walters on national TV that he scared the beejeebies out of her. Then she divorced him, asking for nothing . . . except $125 million for libeling her.

For the record: On "20/20" lovely Robin said, "Michael is a manic-depressive. He is. That's just a fact . . . [He's] scary . . . [He gets] out of control, throwing, screaming. He shakes. He pushes. He swings. And just recently I've become afraid. I mean very very much afraid."

☆ **Getting There:** The mansion is in Bernardsville. See page 38 for address.

MIKE'S BEST PUNCH

It wasn't against Michael Spinks or Mitch Green or any of the myriad chumps who climbed in the ring with him. It was against—guess who?—lovely Robin. Jose Torres in his book *Fire & Fear* quotes Tyson as saying "Man, I'll never forget that punch. . . . She really offended me and I went bam. She flew backward hitting every f— wall in the apartment. That was the best punch I've ever thrown in my f— life."

☆ **Getting There:** That apartment was on Manhattan's East Side. It was in the building at 245 East 40th St.

DRIVING SCHOOL

In the Battle of the Overmuscled Athletes Who Can't Drive, Mike Tyson jumped out to an early lead with his tree crash (see page 37).

But Jose Canseco came roaring back, literally, when he was clocked in excess of 140 mph on a Miami expressway. Canseco cemented his lead with multiple tickets in Arizona during spring training 1989.

But Tyson regained the lead in late spring 1989 when he was ticketed twice in nine days for speeding down Albany, New York's Central Avenue. On April 26, 1989, he was driving his 1989 Lamborghini 71 mph in a 30-mph zone while drag racing a friend. On May 5 he was ticketed again. This time he wasn't clocked but the officer said Tyson was driving in excess of the speed limit.

☆ **Getting There:**
- The Canseco chase began on I-95 in Broward County, Florida, continued into Dade County, and ended when Jose was stopped on the Dolphin Parkway.

- In Scottsdale, Arizona, Canseco was stopped in front of the A's hotel, the Doubletree Suites, 7353 East Indian School Rd., for running a red light, driving without registration, driving without a license, and driving without a license plate. The next day he drove his car to practice anyway. Didn't have any other way to get there, he said.

- Tyson was nabbed the first time at the intersection of Central Ave. and Everett St. in Albany. The second time it was on Central near Tremont.

LOVE THOSE KENNEDYS!

—

America has had a number of great dynasties.

The Adams family gave us John Adams (our second President), John Quincy Adams, (our sixth President), and "The Adams Chronicles" (hit PBS miniseries).

The Roosevelts gave us Teddy (our twenty-sixth President), Franklin (our thirty-second), and "Franklin and Eleanor" (hit ABC miniseries).

And the Sheens have given us Martin (*Apocalypse Now*), Charlie (*Wall Street*), and Emilio (Estevez).

But no family has ever captured our imaginations like the Kennedys.

JOE AND GLORIA

Patriarch Joseph Kennedy and actress Gloria Swanson often "met" at her home, Castle Argyle.

☆ **Getting There:** It was at 1919 Argyle in Hollywood. From the Hollywood Freeway, take Gower St. north to Franklin.

Go left on Franklin. It's three blocks to Argyle. Go right on Argyle.

JFK's PLAYPEN

During the late fifties swinging Senator John F. Kennedy maintained a suite on the eighth floor of Washington's Mayflower Hotel for "personal use." The FBI referred to it as "JFK's playpen." You can figure out what it was for.

☆ **Getting There:** The Mayflower is at 1127 Connecticut Ave. NW, four blocks from the White House. JFK rented Room 812. For reservations call (202) 347-3000.

THEN WHY WAS NIXON THE ONE WHO WAS SWEATING?

JFK supposedly bedded a prostitute minutes before his first debate with Nixon in 1960.

☆ **Getting There:** Kennedy was staying at the Conrad Hilton in Chicago (the site of the first debate), but his tryst happened at the Palmer House, 17 E. Monroe St. From I-90, exit on Monroe St.; the hotel is at the corner of State and Monroe (one block from Michigan Ave). Reservations are (800) HILTONS.

UNDERCOVER COP

Angie Dickinson is best remembered for her years on TV's "Police Woman." But now she has become famous for some undercover work she may have done with JFK. In his book about Jacqueline Kennedy Onassis, *A Woman Called Jackie,* C. David Heymann says that on Inaugural Night JFK slipped away from the party at the Statler Hilton to go upstairs to Frank Sinatra's suite for a half-hour quickie with Angie. Ms. Dickinson has refused to confirm. Or deny.

☆ **Getting There:** The Statler Hilton is now called the Capital Hilton. It's at Sixteenth and K streets NW.

JUDY, JACK. JACK, JUDY

The link between organized crime and the highest levels of US government was a heavily mascaraed divorcée named Judy Campbell, who was sleeping with JFK and mobster Sam Giancana at the same time. (Time frame, not the same bed). Party girl Campbell was introduced to JFK by singer Frank Sinatra in the Sands Lounge of the Las Vegas Sands Hotel in 1960.

☆ **Getting There:** The Sands is the same place it has always been, on the Strip, 3355 Las Vegas Blvd. South. What's new since 1960 is the gigantic Mirage Casino and Hotel across the street and the Fashion Show Mall a block away. The Sands Lounge is at the back of the lobby, past all the slots and gaming tables. The lounge is now the home of a risqué beach show. At least it isn't a nudie ice show.

CHAPPAQUIDDICK

In the early seventies *The National Lampoon* ran a spoof ad of a Volkswagen floating on water and a headline that said, "If Ted Kennedy had been driving a VW, he might be president today." It was a takeoff on VW's ads at the time touting the floatability of the bug. And it was in terrible taste and the magazine later apologized for it.

The event that sparked the spoof ad was the mysterious Chappaquiddick Incident of July 18, 1969. Sometime after midnight Ted Kennedy drove his 1967 Oldsmobile off Dike Bridge on Dike Road, a narrow mud patch that led from Main Street. His companion, unmarried campaign worker Mary Jo Kopechne, drowned. (Years later it was reported she had no underpants on at the time of the drowning.) Kennedy didn't report the incident for eight hours. And the resulting negative publicity has haunted him ever since.

☆ **Getting There:** Chappaquiddick Island is off Martha's Vineyard, which is an island in the Nantucket Sound. There's a passenger ferry from Hyannisport, Massachusetts, and from Quisset, Massachusetts.

Edgartown Town Dock is at the foot of Daggett St., and the On Time car ferry goes to Chappaquiddick.

Here's the route the Kennedy-Kopechne car took that night as testified to by Teddy:

"I was driving my car on Main St. on my way to get to the ferry back to Edgartown. I was unfamiliar with the road and turned right onto Dike Road instead of bearing hard left on Main St. After proceeding for approximately one-half mile on Dike Road I descended a hill and came upon a narrow bridge. The car went off the [right] side of the bridge. . . ."

After the incident, Kennedy swam across the channel and went to his room at the Shiretown Inn in Edgartown. At the front desk he borrowed a dime from the clerk so he could call his girlfriend, an airline stewardess. He didn't tell her about the accident.

Mary Jo Kopechne was staying in Room 56 at the Katama Shores Motor Inn in Edgartown.

Shiretown Inn is at 21 North Water Street, Edgartown, Massachusetts. Katama Shores Motor Inn is at R. F. D. 272, Edgartown, Massachusetts. Take Route 3 south to Cape Cod; use the Bourne Bridge (Exit 6-A). Once you get to Cape Cod, take Route 28 south to Woods Hole and follow the signs to Quisset.

JACKIE OOOO

In 1979, shortly after she turned fifty, former first lady Jackie O had a face-lift, er, "cosmetic surgery in the eye region." It was performed by noted New York plastic surgeon John Conley (who is not the same John Conlee who sings country songs or the same John Connally who was governor of Texas and sitting in the front seat of the limousine in November 1963) at St. Vincent's Hospital in Greenwich Village. She showed up early in the morning wearing no makeup, registered under a false name, and was never discovered until ace biographer C. David Heymann uncovered the story for his biography *A Woman Called Jackie.*

☆ **Getting There:** St. Vincent's Hospital is at 153 West 12th St. in Manhattan.

DR. FEELGOOD

Not feeling chipper today? Got just the thing for you. Throat sore and raspy? Got just the thing for you. Tired blood? Got just the thing for you. No matter what ailed you, Manhattan physician Dr. Max Jacobson had just the thing for you: an injection of vitamins and amphetamines. That's how he acquired the nickname Dr. Feelgood.

The good doctor supplied his "feelgood" treatments to a number of celebrities during the sixties and early seventies, from JFK and Jackie to Judy Garland, Eddie Fisher, Tennessee Williams, even Winston Churchill.

☆ **Getting There:** Dr. Feelgood's office was at 155 East 72nd St. in New York.

MARILYN

—

When a friend says something about Marilyn, do you think he's talking about the Vice President's wife? If so, skip to the next chapter.

Marilyn means only Marilyn Monroe. Just as they retired her one-time husband Joe DiMaggio's number, so too should they retire her name. No more Marilyns please. Marilyn Monroe is the one.

—

SOME LIKE IT HOT

If you've seen *The Seven-Year Itch*, you've never forgotten the image. Even if you've only seen the poster, you've probably never forgotten it, it's that memorable. The scene: Marilyn Monroe and Tom Ewell have come out of the movie theater after watching *The Creature from the Black Lagoon* (she says she just felt so sorry for the creature at the end) and are heading up New York City's Lexington Avenue when a subway goes under the street and a puff of air inflates her skirt. "Oh, do you feel the breeze from the subway?" she coos. And everyone in the audience melts when she adds, "Isn't it delicious?"

☆ **Getting There:** The scene was filmed at the subway grate on Lexington Ave. at Fifty-fifth St., outside of what used to be the Trans-Lux Theater. It's now a giant office building.

GENTLEMEN PREFER BLONDES

It has to be the most famous calendar in American history, which may tell you more about American history than it does about the calendar. It is the well-known nude calendar of soon-to-be superstar Marilyn Monroe. She posed for commercial photographer Tom Kelley on May 27, 1949, in a garage studio at 736 North Seward in Los Angeles. Later, when asked what she had on, she replied, "The radio."

Actually she had the record player on. Kelley's wife played Artie Shaw's "Begin the Beguine" over and over to relax Marilyn. Monroe was paid $50 for the session. Kelley later sold the photos to a Chicago calendar company for $500. The company sold eight million calendars.

☆ **Getting There:** In Los Angeles take the Melrose Ave. exit from the Hollywood Freeway. Go west past the Paramount Studios. Seward is four blocks past Cahuenga Blvd. Go right on Seward.

THE MISFIT

Marilyn died alone in her modest bungalow, victim of a drug overdose. Or a hit ordered by Robert Kennedy, depending on whom you believe.

☆ **Getting There:** The address is 12305 Fifth Helena Dr. From the San Diego Freeway, take Sunset Blvd. west to Helena. Go left to Fifth. The window just to the left of the door was the bedroom where she OD'd.

For more on Marilyn, see Dangerous Liaisons, page 75.

ELVIS IS STILL THE KING . . . AND STILL DEAD

▬

They don't have any shame in Memphis when it comes
to Elvis. If you got the money, honey, they will sell
you everything from Elvis shampoo to Elvis sweat. And
when it comes to sights, they show it all. His gaudy tiger-
print Jungle Room, his tacky private jet, his flashy car collection. Still they draw the line when it comes to a few
things. We cross that line . . .

ELVIS'S DRUGSTORE

On the day before he died Elvis received 150 tablets and
200 cubic centimeters of the painkillers Percodan and
Dilaudid, 262 pills of the depressants Amytal and Quaa-
lude, and 278 tablets of the stimulants Dexedrine and Bi-
phetamine. Elvis's medicine cabinet *was* a drugstore.

But in fact many of Elvis's drugs were purchased at
Prescription House, a Memphis drugstore that was identi-
fied as a major supplier of Elvis's drugs in the 1981 trial of
Elvis's doctor, George Nichopoulos, who was accused of

49

overprescribing drugs for Elvis, Jerry Lee Lewis, and nine others, including Nichopoulos himself. He was later acquitted.

In 1980 Jack Kirsch, owner of Prescription House, had pleaded no contest to charges of filling 175 Presley prescriptions for a total of 11,000 pills.

☆ **Getting There:** Prescription House is at 1800 Union Ave. in Memphis. It identifies itself in the Memphis Yellow Pages as "Your discount pharmacy specializing in compounding dermatology prescriptions." In downtown Memphis, take Exit 30, the Union Ave. exit, east from I-240.

ELVIS'S DOCTOR

Dr. George Nichopoulos, Dr. Nick as Elvis affectionately called him, and with good reason, prescribed 5,300 uppers, downers, and painkillers for Elvis in the last seven months of his life.

☆ **Getting There:** Dr. Nick's office was at 6027 Walnut Grove Rd. in Memphis. There is a Walnut Grove Rd. exit from I-240, just south of its intersection with I-40. Take it east about five blocks. Dr. Nick's office is near Baptist Hospital East.

ELVIS'S DRY OUTS

Although it was denied vehemently at the time, the real reason Elvis checked into the hospital in 1973, 1975, and 1977 wasn't "exhaustion." It was to dry out. His dry-out spot of choice was Memphis's Baptist Memorial Hospital. In April 1977 he occupied a two-room suite on the sixteenth floor. In January 1975 he was on the eighteenth floor. His first dry out, in October 1973, was on the sixteenth floor.

☆ **Getting There:** Baptist Memorial Hospital Medical Center is at 899 Madison Ave., in Memphis. The phone is (901)

522-5252. Take Interstate 240 toward downtown. Go west on Madison Ave.

ELVIS '88: THE KING IN KALAMAZOO

In 1988, for some reason, people all across America got the idea that Elvis wasn't really dead, that he had faked his death to get a little peace and quiet, and that he had actually spent the previous eleven years enjoying himself, wandering the country, seducing fat waitresses who knew who he was but decided not to tell until the *Weekly World News* called.

He was spotted in Georgia and in Germany; in Texas and in Tennessee. But the majority of the sightings centered in the Kalamazoo, Michigan, area.

Why Elvis? Why Kalamazoo, Michigan?

We investigated.

Let's begin with a song:

> *Elvis has five letters.*
> *Jesus has five letters.*
> *Elvis and Jesus are both Capricorns.*
> *Jesus was a carpenter.*
> *Elvis was an electrician.*
> *Is it just a coincidence?*

—From a song disc jockeys Bob Moody and Gary Burbank are writing.

Moody and Burbank were playing off the headlines, the headlines in the supermarket tabloids, in their little song that implied that if Jesus could come back from the dead then, by God, so could Elvis.

The Elvis Is Alive mania began the last week in May 1988 when the *Weekly World News* broke the story: "After faking his tragic death [in 1977], exhausted idol Elvis Presley was secretly flown to Hawaii, where he began his new life under the name John Burrows."

The newspaper quoted from a new book *Is Elvis Alive? The Most Incredible Elvis Presley Story Ever Told,* by author Gail Brewer-Giorgio, who—just coincidentally —also wrote the novel *Orion,* about a rock star who faked his own death. The Elvis book came complete with an audiocassette tape of conversations with Elvis *after* his death.

"Everything worked just like it was meant to be," E said on the secret tape. "There was an island I had learned about a long time ago. I must have spent a year there. I really needed the rest."

Voice analyst Len Williams, of Houston, verified that the voice on the tape was Elvis's, and that the tape had been edited. Brewer-Giorgio shrugged that one off, saying it was edited to take out the voice of the person talking with Elvis.

So how had Elvis been since his death? "It's been enjoyable, but it's been a constant battle, growing a beard and this and that, to keep from being recognized. . . . I'm hoping that a lot of people out there are not disappointed with me. I mean, I didn't mean to put anybody through any pain. It's taken a lot to have to do what I had to do. But in the long run it's going to pay off."

The tape was supposedly made in 1981. Elvis said he hadn't had a sleeping pill in three years and didn't like the films about him. He said he plans to come out when "the time is right."

Soon America's tabloids were swamped with tales from chubby waitresses who had lived with Elvis and pimply faced teenagers who saw someone who looked like him at the local hamburger heaven.

In the June 28, 1988, issue of the supermarket tabloid *Weekly World News,* amid such headlines as "Space Aliens Graveyard Found!" and "Man Keeps Wife's Body in Freezer for 23 Years!" and "Cheeseburger Kills Space Alien!" was this shocker:

I'VE SEEN ELVIS AND HE'S ALIVE AND WELL!
Woman spots Presley at a Kalamazoo Burger King

The diligence of *Weekly World*'s reporters had turned up an eyewitness, Louise Welling, fifty-one, a Kalamazoo,

Michigan, housewife, who said she saw Elvis twice: in September she had gone to Felpausch's grocery in suburban Vicksburg, Michigan, after church, and spotted him in the next checkout lane. He was buying a fuse. "He was dressed in an all-white jumpsuit and holding a motorcycle helmet," she said. "He'd lost weight, and he didn't have sideburns."

She spotted him a second time two months later at the J. C. Penney entrance of the Crossroads Mall. And in May her children saw Elvis in a red Ferrari at a Burger King drive-through window.

Was Elvis alive?

And if so, why hadn't he had a hit lately?

I conducted my own investigation.

The first thing I had to answer was: why Kalamazoo?

Why did Elvis Presley, Tupelo, Mississippi, native and longtime Memphis, Tennessee, resident, pick Kalamazoo for his hideaway?

I had no clue. I didn't even know where Kalamazoo was.

So to help unravel the mystery, I sent for the Kalamazoo Chamber of Commerce's newcomer guide. I assume Elvis must have done this in those hectic last days before his death.

Here's what I—and Elvis—learned:

Kalamazoo, which is an Indian name meaning "mirage of reflecting river," is halfway between Chicago and Detroit, about three hours from each.

It is "becoming an important center for business, education, culture . . . [has a] strong and dependable work force . . . [and] innovative and responsible leadership."

There are a lot of lakes and golf courses nearby, none of which would have much appeal for Elvis.

There are five malls.

Kalamazoo boasts that it is "the leading center for the arts in southwest Michigan," again no appeal for Elvis.

The average January temperature is 24 degrees; the average July temperature is 79 degrees. It is a much colder place than Memphis, although summers are more moderate.

But Elvis never gave any indication he wanted a colder climate. He vacationed in Hawaii and Palm Springs.

There are 250 churches representing fifty denominations, a plus for Elvis, but there are many communities in this country with just as many churches.

For a TV hound like Elvis there are three network affiliates, plus PBS and a cable system. But satellite dishes make all that irrelevant. He could get his television anywhere.

Elvis was a big sports fan. Could it be the sports environment, I wondered?

But Kalamazoo is a big tennis and ice-hockey town. There's the top-rated college ice-hockey team at Western Michigan University. There is the annual National Boys Tennis Championship.

And Kalamazoo's two pro teams are the Wings of the International Hockey League and the Kangaroos of the American Indoor Soccer Association. Elvis did ice skate, but there are no indications he ever went to an ice-hockey match. And, when he was growing up, soccer was considered part of the world communist conspiracy.

So what was it about Kalamazoo, I kept asking myself?

The annual Flowerfest in July, designed to showcase Kalamazoo County as the "nation's largest producer of bedding plants?" Nah.

The Kalamazoo Air Zoo, with old planes, an annual air show and trade expo? Nah.

The annual Michigan Wine & Harvest Festival in September? Maybe.

The 640 acres of trails and botanical gardens at the Kalamazoo Nature center? The Kellogg Bird Sanctuary? The NASA/Michigan space center?

Terrific stuff, for sure, but nothing Elvis would have cared about.

I couldn't find any plausible explanation until I spotted a short paragraph on the back of the Kalamazoo County "Come and see our corner of Michigan" brochure. It leaped out at me:

"Kalamazoo County . . . is the world headquarters of the Upjohn Company, and you can take a fascinating tour of their pharmaceutical production facility."

Bingo.

☆ Getting There:

- The Kalamazoo Burger King where Elvis was spotted is at 3015 South Westnedge Ave. Take Westnedge Ave. exit south from Interstate 94.

- Felpausch's grocery, which was Harding's when Welling saw Elvis, is at 120 West Prairie in Vicksburg, Michigan. From I-94 take 131 South to V. W. Avenue. Take a left on V. W. Avenue, which will take you all the way into Vicksburg (about five miles). V. W. Avenue becomes West Prairie.

- The J. C. Penney entrance of the Crossroads Mall. Crossroads Mall is at the corner of Westnedge Ave. and Romence Rd. Take Westnedge Ave. exit south from Interstate 94 to the Mall Ring Rd. J. C. Penney's is on the north side of the mall.

- Welling also said Elvis was living in the Columbia Plaza Hotel under the name John Burrows. She said she called there several times and asked for Burrows and each time was told he was out to lunch at Wendy's. The Columbia Plaza is at 350 East Michigan Ave. in Kalamazoo's historic Haymarket district. The Wendy's is at 305 East Michigan Ave., a block down. Go north on Westnedge, past Upjohn Park, and turn right on Michigan Ave.

- Upjohn Pharmaceuticals is at 7171 Portage Rd. Sad to say the company no longer offers tours.

ELVIS LIVES AGAIN!

Just when you thought it was safe to read a supermarket tabloid again, the *National Examiner* was back on the Elvis Lives story. E had been spotted living on a farm near Cleveland, Alabama. He'd even been glimpsed at the local

Where Elvis shot out a TV set.

pharmacy and at the Dogwood Inn in Oneonta, Alabama. He was using the name Johnny Buford during his Alabama sojourn.

☆ **Getting There:** The Dogwood Inn is at 301 First Ave. East, Oneonta, Alabama. Directions: Take 75 into town and make a right at the second light.

The pharmacist at the Cleveland pharmacy where Elvis was spotted says that Buford came forth and said his real name was Tommy Johns. Not Elvis.

WHERE ELVIS SHOT OUT A TV SET

Elvis hated Robert Goulet. Detested him.

But then again don't we all?

Anytime he saw Goulet on TV, he became violently angry. Unfortunately, in the days when Mike Douglas and Merv Griffin ruled the afternoon airwaves, Goulet was on TV a lot. Elvis shot up the TV with Goulet on it several times, usually in his suite at the Las Vegas Hilton Hotel. The most famous time Elvis pulled a derringer out of his boot and fired it into the set, sending sparks everywhere.

Elvis didn't limit his gunplay to shooting up TV sets.

He shot up lots of small appliances and a few large ones. In February 1974, he fired at a light switch in his Vegas suite. The bullet penetrated the wall and just missed his girlfriend at the time, Linda Thompson. She came running into his room trembling, but Elvis was able to soothe her by saying, "Hey now, hon, just don't get excited."

From then on he confined his shooting to the TV and the chandelier, explaining to his boys, "We're in the penthouse. Nobody's gonna get hit long as you shoot straight up."

☆ **Getting There:** Las Vegas Hilton is at the corner of Flamingo Rd. and Las Vegas Blvd. (The Strip!) in Las Vegas, Nevada. Take the Flamingo Rd. exit, Exit 38, from I-15. Elvis stayed in the four-bedroom presidential suite on the thirtieth floor; it's right under the word *Hilton*. It's now known as the Presley Suite. As recently as 1983, when I was there for a convention, there was a bullet hole in a door frame. The bullet hole has been fixed. For reservations call (702) 732-5111.

ELVIS'S DOG'S HOSPITAL ROOM

In 1975 Elvis's chow, Get-Lo, was in bad shape. His kidneys were failing so Elvis had him flown to Boston for treatment. Get-Lo wasn't strong enough to make the fifty-mile trip to the New England Institute of Comparative Medicine in West Boylston, Massachusetts, so Elvis had him put up at the Copley Plaza Hotel in Boston, and doctors from the Institute came to him. They determined that neither dialysis nor a transplant was needed, gave Get-Lo fluid treatments, and sent him home. A few months later Get-Lo died.

☆ **Getting There:** The Copley Plaza Hotel is at 138 St. James Ave. in Boston. From the Massachusetts Turnpike take Dartmouth St. north two blocks to St. James. Turn right to Copley Square. For reservations call (800) 225-7654.

ELVIS MAYOR

Bruce Borders, the mayor of Jasonville, Indiana, is America's only Elvis impersonator mayor.

☆ **Getting There:** Jasonville is about half an hour south of Terre Haute. From US 41-150 take state Route 48 east. It's about twelve miles.

COUSINS, IDENTICAL COUSINS

———

The Strange, Intertwisted Fates of Cousins Mickey Gilley, Jerry Lee Lewis, and Jimmy Swaggart

Ferriday, Louisiana, looks like every other sleepy Southern town: a tumble-down main street with video stores where dry goods shops once reigned, a back street where old men gather to whittle and talk politics, and a Wal-Mart out on the edge of town. But the welcoming sign lets you know this town is different:

WELCOME TO FERRIDAY
HOME OF MICKEY GILLEY, EDWARD K. SMITH, JERRY LEE
LEWIS, JIMMY SWAGGART, AND MRS. U.B. EVANS, NATIONALLY
KNOWN HORTICULTURIST

Actually that's what it used to say. They've painted over the parts about Mickey, Jerry Lee, Jimmy, and Ed Smith. So that makes Ferriday the Former Home of Jerry Lee Lewis, Mickey Gilley, Ed Smith, and Jimmy Swag-

Former birthplace of Jerry Lee Lewis, Jimmy Swaggart, and Mickey Gilley.

gart. They've been disowned. (I think Ed was an innocent victim: he just happened to be on the scroll-part under Jerry Lee.)

That one state could produce three such oddities as Jerry Lee, Jimmy, and Mickey would be enough, but that the three came from the same tiny town, all three born there within a twelve-month period, is unbelievable. Before you start thinking it's in the water, think again. The three are first cousins. It's in the blood.

MICKEY

Mickey Gilley became the hero of every closet country music lover when his gargantuan Pasadena, Texas, night-club served as the backdrop for the John Travolta movie *Urban Cowboy*. Gilley's meant uptown Texas-style country music, and the movie gave Gilley a big chart-crossing hit, "Stand By Me." When people heard anything about Gilley's, its mechanical bull, its nightly hoedown, they immediately thought of Mickey.

Now Mickey had tasted stardom before *Urban Cow-*

boy. He'd had number-one country hits and he'd won awards. In 1976 he was the Academy of Country Music's Entertainer of the Year, Male Vocalist of the Year, and his songs won Single of the Year, Album of the Year, and Song of the Year. But stardom is one thing; superstardom is another. His cousin Jerry Lee was a superstar. His cousin Jimmy was a superstar. Mickey was a star.

Suddenly Mickey had a shot at the top. All he needed to do was capitalize on the megapopularity of *Urban Cowboy*.

So what does he do? He busts up with his longtime club partner and sues to get his name removed from the club. And wins.

The place is closed now.

You're pushing your luck, Mickey.

☆ **Getting There:** Gilley's was at 4500 Spencer Highway in Pasadena, Texas, a suburb of Houston. From I-45 take South Shaver to Pasadena. It intersects with Spencer Highway. Go right (east) on Spencer.

JIMMY

"Jimmy to us was like Jesus walking on the face of the earth again."—his cousin Mickey Gilley.

When he gave up his pulpit on February 21, 1988, Jimmy Swaggart was the United States' most-watched televangelist. He was religion's Mick Jagger, a dancing, weeping, crying, screaming, singing preacher-performer, whose daily performances built a $142-million-a-year ministry.

But apparently there was another Jimmy Swaggart, one who not only didn't like to perform, he refused to perform. He only wanted to watch. His voyeurism cost him his throne when in the spring of 1988 rival evangelist Marvin Gorman, whom Swaggart had driven into bankruptcy with charges of sexual infidelities, extracted his revenge. Complete with photos.

Jimmy Swaggart had been spending time down on

New Orleans's Airline Highway, a neon jungle of no-tell motels. Gorman had photos of Swaggart and a tattooed harlot named Debra Murphree exiting from Room 7 of the Travel Inn, where she had been engaged in posing for his preying eyes.

Jimmy fell from grace at this seedy hot-sheets motel parked underneath a billboard warning YOUR ETERNITY IS AT STAKE.

So Jimmy gave up his Assembly of God credentials.

But that wasn't the end of Jimmy the preacher. After a suitable period of penitence, say twelve weeks, Jimmy was back on the air with his own denomination. Welcome home, James.

GREAT MOMENTS IN JIMMY LEE SWAGGART HISTORY

Where Jimmy Swaggart Found God In front of the Arcade Theater on Louisiana Avenue in Ferriday, Louisiana.

While standing in line to get a ticket during the summer of 1944, he heard a voice call out, "Do not go in this place. I have chosen you as a vessel to be in my service." Swaggart soon began preaching at the Assembly of God church. (While in Ferriday, you might also want to stop by City Hall and talk to Ferriday Mayor Sammy Davis, Jr. No relation.)

☆ **Getting There:** State Route 568 is Louisiana Ave. in Ferriday. The Arcade is one block north of the intersection with 84.

Where Jimmy Fell from Grace Room 7 of the Travel Inn at 1131 Airline Highway in New Orleans. According to *Penthouse* you can see inside for only $13 an hour, $16 for three hours. That's the going rate for anyone, not just tourists. And POSITIVELY NO REFUNDS AFTER THE FIRST FIFTEEN MINUTES.

☆ **Getting There:** Take the Airline Highway exit from Highway 10 (you can only go one way), and the Travel Inn will be about a quarter of a mile.

JERRY LEE

There's not much to write about the Killer that hasn't already been written. Suffice to say what is a sin to Jimmy is an everyday happenstance to Jerry Lee.

GREAT MOMENTS IN JERRY LEE LEWIS HISTORY

Where He Tried to Kill His Sister His family lived in Angola, Louisiana, for a short time and it was while there, in 1948, that twelve-year-old Jerry Lee figured out a way to get rid of his bratty three-year-old sister for all time. According to Nick Tosches in *Hellfire*, Jerry Lee put little Frankie Jean in the baby stroller, took her out to a new construction site, and shoved her over the cliff. When he got home, his mama asked where Frankie Jean was. Twice. The second time, Jerry Lee finally responded: "A chicken hawk. Biggest one I ever seen. Snatched her up like a poor little chickling hen and carried her off. Stroller and all." (She wasn't seriously injured.)

☆ **Getting There:** They were living in a small house outside the Louisiana State Prison where Jerry Lee's daddy was working construction. The building is gone and so is the cliff, which was part of construction. But it is near where the prison hospital is today. From Baton Rouge go north on US 61 to SR 66. Follow it around to Tunica and Angola.

Where He Preached In 1952 Jerry Lee came up with the strange notion that he was going to be a preacher. He preached occasionally at the Assembly of God church at 100 Cypress Avenue in Ferriday, but that lasted about as long as his marriage.

☆ **Getting There:** From downtown go north on SR 15 and turn right just past Taunton's Ferriday Superette. It will take you over to the church.

Where He Sinned Author Nick Tosches, in *Hellfire*, quotes Jerry Lee as saying Miss Nelle Jackson's at 416 North Rankin Street in Natchez, Mississippi, was "the greatest whorehouse in the south." There was even a wooden leg above the door, a reminder to all about the customer who didn't want to pay.

☆ **Getting There:** In Natchez, Jerry Lee's whorehouse is at the corner of Monroe and Rankin. Rankin is one way south, so from US 61 Business take Pine to Monroe or Union to Madison. It's a large rambling white house with a picket fence in front. And it's no longer a whorehouse.

Where He Met the Twelve-Year-Old Cousin Who Would Become His Third Wife (while he was still married to number two) and whose existence would wreck his British tour. Myra Gale was twelve at the time they met and still living at home with her parents. Her father, J. W. Brown, was Jerry Lee's daddy's sister's son, making Myra Gale Jerry Lee's first cousin, once removed. The Browns lived at 4908 East Shore Drive in Memphis.

☆ **Getting There:** From US 61 south of town take Shelby Dr. east to East Shore Dr. Go south.

Where He Married His Thirteen-year-old Cousin Myra Gale Brown and Jerry Lee Lewis were wed on Dec. 12, 1957, at the wedding chapel in Hernando, Mississippi. It was formerly the Spencer house.

☆ **Getting There:** The Spencer house burned several years ago. It was at the corner of Highway 51 and Holly Springs St. It's now a Quick Shop market.

Where He Shot His Bass Player On September 29, 1976, bass player Butch Owens was visiting Jerry Lee at 435 Cardinal Drive in Memphis when Jerry Lee told Owens he was going to shoot a Co-Cola bottle over Owens's shoulder. Two .357 Magnum shells entered Owens's chest. Jerry Lee was later charged with shooting a firearm in the city limits, a misdemeanor. He told police it was an accident.

☆ **Getting There:** It's in Collierville, southeast of Memphis. From US 57 (Poplar St.) turn left on Shelby Dr. and go two blocks to Cardinal Dr.

Say Hi to Frankie Jean If you visit Ferriday, don't miss Frankie Jean's drive-through grocery store. Frankie Jean is there most of the time.

☆ **Getting There:** Frankie Jean's Pik Quik drive-through grocery is on SR 15 west of "downtown," right across from Taunton's Ferriday Superette.

ROCK AND ROLL IS HERE TO STAY

—

And so are the strange tales of rock and roll excess. Tales like these . . .

—

JAWS

The story has achieved legendary status. It has been repeated so often that nobody believes it anymore. But it's true, according to *Hammer of the Gods*, Stephen Davis's history of the rock group Led Zeppelin. It happened in May 1969 during the group's second American tour. Members of the group were fishing from their hotel balcony, caught a shark, and used it to perform unnatural sex acts with a groupie.

(Richard Cole, the group's manager at the time, says in *Hammer of the Gods* that it was actually a red snapper and it was Cole who initiated the sex scene.)

☆ **Getting There:** The most famous rock star party happened at the Edgewater Inn in Seattle. It's at 2411 Alaska Way, Pier 67.

WHO ARE YOU?

The biggest party boys in all of rock were the members of The Who. And the biggest party boy in The Who was the late Keith Moon. If it could be done to or in a hotel room, he did it.

☆ **Getting There:** In the Hotel Navarro in New York, Keith Moon cut a hole from one room to the next so he could get a record player. The Hotel Navarro was at 112 Central Park South. It's now the Ritz-Carlton.

At the Holiday Inn in Flint, Michigan, he celebrated his birthday with a birthday-suit swim in the pool and a cake fight. The Holiday Inn was at 2207 West Bristol Rd. and I-75. It's now the Days Inn.

SHUT DOWN

James Watt was Secretary of the Interior for a brief non-shining moment in the early eighties. Among his many accomplishments, which included selling off mineral rights in national forests, was the banning of the Beach Boys from performing on the Washington Mall. You might excuse his behavior, thinking perhaps he had them confused with the more strident Beastie Boys, except that at the time the Beastie Boys were still in grade school.

☆ **Getting There:** The Washington Mall is that two-mile expanse of grass between the Lincoln Memorial and the Capitol.

THE DEVIL'S WOODSTOCK

The music festival at the Altamont Motor Speedway in California was only four months after Woodstock, but just as Woodstock has come to symbolize all that peace-love-dove stuff, so has Altamont come to mark the end of innocence (or the end of *the* innocence, if you are a

Don Henley fan). During the Rolling Stones' performance a member of the Hell's Angel motorcycle gang, which had been hired to provide security, stabbed to death eighteen-year-old Meredith Hunter, who had pulled a gun.

For years there has been controversy over what the Stones were singing at the time of the stabbing. Was it "Sympathy for the Devil"? Or . . .

I'm here to settle that controversy. It doesn't matter what the Stones were singing at the time.

☆ **Getting There:** Altamont Motor Speedway no longer exists. Where it used to be: Altamont Pass is on Interstate 580 between Tracy and Livermore. It's currently private property covered with hundreds and hundreds of windmills.

R-E-S-P-E-C-T: FIND OUT WHAT IT MEANS TO ARETHA

The woman who made a fortune spelling "respect" didn't have much of that trait for her old neighbors after she moved up in style. Aretha Franklin's old middle-class house sits condemned, grass up to the window ledges. Aretha bought the house in 1967, about the time her hit "Respect" was moving up the charts, and lived there five years before turning it over to her grandmother, who lived there until 1982. It's been vacant ever since and the neighbors are fuming about it. "She has given us no respect," neighbor Millicent Lewis told *People*. The neighbors sued Aretha in small claims court for $1,500, claiming she had hurt their property values by abandoning her house. The case is still in court at this writing.

Aretha now lives in chic Bloomfield Hills, Michigan.

☆ **Getting There:** Aretha's old house is at 19346 Sorrento Ave. in Detroit. From SR 10 take Vassar Dr. east to Sorrento and take Sorrento north.

WHERE MADONNA LOST HER DRESS

Too bad: she wasn't in it at the time. Actually it was part of a traveling mall exhibit, MTV's Museum of Unnatural History, when a Novi, Michigan, teenager swiped Madonna's gorgeous frock right off the traveling mannequin in July 1988. It was the True Blue dress, the one Madonna had worn in her "True Blue" video. MTV officials estimated its value at $20,000. Sure.

Police in Novi had some help in solving the case. A group of high school kids spotted a woman pinching the dress and chased her. She dumped the hot frock in a bush, where the teens found it. They kept it until they read in the paper about its reputed value.

☆ **Getting There:** The Twelve Oaks Mall in Novi is at 27500 Novi Rd. Take I-275 north (from Detroit) to I-96 west. Exit 162 and turn right; the mall is right there.

STICKING IT OUT IN MIAMI

As the Doors' popularity increased, so did lead singer Jim Morrison's drinking. And during a March 1969 concert in Miami, he did the unthinkable. He dropped his pants, exposing himself, then made masturbatory motions.

Or did he? Morrison maintained he didn't. At his trial, his defense team called a stream of witnesses who said he didn't. But the jury couldn't make up its mind. In the end the jury found him not guilty of the felony charge of lewd and lascivious behavior but guilty of the misdemeanor charge of exposing himself. Morrison was given a jail term but died while the case was being appealed.

☆ **Getting There:** The concert was March 1, 1969, in a converted airplane hangar called Dinner Key Auditorium in Miami. It was at 3360 Pan American Dr. It is now the Coconut Grove Exhibition Center.

PARTY TIME

―――

What would our paparazzi do if not for parties? Hang out outside the Rolls dealerships? Fortunately our celebrities love parties and party time.

―――

THE PLACE TO HAVE BEEN

Remember the photos? A mob of young adults, screaming at the burly doorman, offering favors of all sorts if he would just let them inside.

It was Studio 54, the hottest of the hot nightclubs. Mick and Bianca went there. So did Truman Capote and Liza Minnelli, Andy Warhol and Margaret Trudeau, every rock star and every vacant model in New York. There was an unsubstantiated report that Jimmy Carter's advisor Hamilton Jordan was seen snorting cocaine there.

It has quite a reputation for a club that was only open for twenty months.

But then owners Steve Rubell and Ian Schrager met their match. Not even the burly doorman could keep the IRS out. And in 1979 they began fifteen-month prison terms for that little "oops, forgot."

Former site of Studio 54: The Ritz.

☆ **Getting There:** Studio 54 was at 254 West 54th St. near Eighth Ave. in Manhattan.

ANOTHER PLACE TO HAVE BEEN

Andy Warhol said it was where pop art and pop life came together. David Bowie remembered meeting Iggy Pop for the first time there in the early seventies. "Me, Iggy, and Lou Reed at one table with nothing to say to each other, just looking at each other's eye makeup." It was Max's Kansas City, and it was the Studio 54 of the sixties.

☆ **Getting There:** It was at 213 Park Ave. South near Eighteenth St. in Manhattan.

UNDER THE MUNCHKINS

If you've seen the movie *Under the Rainbow,* I don't need to say any more than: the Munchkins' hotel. If you don't know about the legend of the little people who played the Munchkins in the 1939 fantasy *The Wizard of Oz,* pull up a chair. Over the years the legend has grown, but even if only one-fourth of it is true, they were quite a colony.

Supposedly the Munchkins were the most playful of people, forever pulling practical jokes on the help and other guests at the Culver City Hotel, where they were boarded during filming. Judy Garland said, "They got smashed every night and the police had to pick them up in butterfly nets." Another story has it that police had to be stationed on every floor to break up their parties.

They reportedly did a few other things too, but this book is PG.

☆ **Getting There:** The Munchkins stayed and played at the Culver City Hotel, 9400 Culver Blvd. From the Santa Monica Freeway (I-10) take Venice Blvd. south until it intersects with Culver Blvd. Go left on Culver.

WAILIN' AND THE BOYS

He's calmed down now; they all have. But in the seventies Waylon Jennings was one hell-raiser. In 1978 he and his band destroyed their rooms at the Little America Hotel in Flagstaff, Arizona. They trashed four rooms, breaking light fixtures, pulling down curtains, and disabling air conditioners by fouling them with sand.

☆ **Getting There:** The Little America Hotel is 2515 East Butler Ave. right off I-40 at Exit 198.

ASSETS

It was a great party while it lasted. But in the end it was the biggest savings and loan failure in the history of the United States. By a long shot. The Vernon Savings and Loan in Vernon, Texas, cost taxpayers $1.3 billion in bailout funds; 95 percent of its loans were uncollectible.

How did they do it? Well, they bought a beach house worth $2 million in Del Mar, California, for owner Don

Ray Dixon to live in rent-free. And they bought $5.5 million in cowboy art. And they paid topless dancer Joy Love (probably not her real name) to entertain a Texas bank examiner who just coincidentally approved the S&L's purchase of a Rolls-Royce dealership and a Ferrari dealership.

According to testimony, prostitutes were procured for the regulator and also for Vernon executives. One Vernon executive tried to avoid conviction by using the novel defense that Ms. Love wasn't really a bribe because the regulator was impotent and therefore couldn't take advantage of Ms. Love's assets.

☆ **Getting There:** Vernon Savings and Loan is now First Gibraltar Savings. It's in Vernon at the corner of Main and Wilbarger streets, on the southwest corner, appropriately enough, right across from the courthouse. The Million Dollar Saloon is at 6826 Greeneville Ave. in Dallas.

RADICAL CHEEK

It was an unusual get-together: the society folks were on one side of the room, the Black Panthers on the other. It was a benefit hosted in 1970 by Mr. and Mrs. Leonard Bernstein to raise bail money for the Panther 21, a group of twenty-one Black Panthers who were charged with conspiring to blow up a number of Manhattan buildings, including the very department stores where many of these society folks shopped.

Among the chic guests were Otto Preminger, Peter Duchin, Barbara Walters, and Charlotte Curtis. The radicals included Robert Bay, forty-one hours away from a guncharge arrest; Don Cox, the Panthers' field marshal; and Henry Miller, the Harlem defense captain.

Writer Tom Wolfe covered the party, and in his article in *New York* magazine labeled this bleeding heart benefit "radical chic." The name, and the shame, stuck.

☆ **Getting There:** The Bernsteins' duplex penthouse apartment was at Park Ave. and Seventy-ninth St.

DANGEROUS LIAISONS

—

Who's zoomin' who? is the way Aretha Franklin puts it. It's a polite way of talking about those dangerous liaisons that famous folk seem to get themselves involved in.

JIM AND JESSICA

It was the Sheraton Sand Key Hotel in Clearwater Beach, Florida, where evangelist Jim Bakker forced himself on church secretary Jessica Hahn. His exact words, according to Hahn, were "Jessica, by helping the shepherd, you're helping the sheep."

☆ **Getting There:** It happened in Room 538 of the Sheraton Sand Key Hotel in Clearwater, Florida. At one time hotel management wanted to change the number of every room on the fifth floor to 538, it was such a popular tourist attraction.

A spokesperson in the executive office said, "People

still ask for it, but it's not like it was." From Tampa, take Highway 60 west to Clearwater Beach. When you see a big Holiday Inn Surfside on the right, turn left at that light. Stay in the right-hand lane and follow that road around (Gulfview Boulevard). You'll soon see several hotels (a Hilton on the end); just bear right over the bridge, and the Sheraton Sand Key Hotel will be just beyond the tollgate.

The address is 1160 Gulf Blvd., Clearwater Beach, Florida. The phone number is (813) 595-1611.

(For more on Hahn's virginity, see Inquiring Minds Want to Go, page 25.)

JACK AND MARILYN

I can remember as a kid watching Marilyn Monroe coo "Happy Birthday" to President Kennedy and thinking, Gee, how nice of her to do that for our President, go all the way to New York just to sing at his birthday party. We now know she did a lot more than just sing.

She also sang "Happy Birthday" to him later that night at the Carlyle Hotel, where he was staying without Jackie.

☆ **Getting There:** The Carlyle Hotel is at 35 East 76th St. in Manhattan. JFK's suite was 34-A, a penthouse duplex that management kept empty for the President's use.

JACK AND MARILYN AGAIN

In California Jack and Marilyn would meet at Peter Lawford's Malibu Beach house.

☆ **Getting There:** It was at 625 Palisades Beach Rd. From the San Diego Freeway (I-405) take Santa Monica Blvd. west until it dead-ends into Ocean Ave. Go right to California Ave. Take a left. It angles down to Palisades Beach Rd. Go right about two blocks. It's on the left, on the ocean.

ROB AND THE CRADLE

It is, to date, his most famous movie. More people have seen it—in clips—than saw *Illegally Yours* and *Masquerade* and *Square Dance,* three of his turkeys, put together. It almost made people forget his embarrassing performance crooning to the trademarked Snow White person on the 1988 Oscar show.

Rob Lowe's 8mm videotape of himself and an unidentified white male having sex with an unidentified white female was shown on "Inside Edition" and "A Current Affair" and "Entertainment Tonight" and even a few local newscasts. And it wasn't even the clip that got him in trouble. *That* clip, of Rob encouraging an underage Atlanta girl and her lesbian companion to show him what girls do to each other, was erased from the tape. But not before the girl's mother filed suit against Rob, claiming he used his celebrity, such as it was, to seduce her daughter when he was in Atlanta to attend the 1988 Democratic National Convention. That case is still in court.

A potential criminal charge—which in Georgia could have brought Lowe thousands of years in prison—was dropped after Lowe agreed to use his celebrity, such as it is, to encourage Los Angeles high school kids not to use drugs.

☆ **Getting There:** Rob met the girl and her friend at Club Rio, a trendy downtown Atlanta bar. It is at the corner of Luckie St. NW and International Blvd. NW, off Techwood Dr. NW. The action took place in Room 2845 of the Atlanta Hilton and Towers, only a few blocks away at the corner of Courtland and Harris NE. For reservations call (800) HILTONS.

PETER AND PASSION FLOWER

Her real name was Romina Danielson but her testimony in the 1987 Joan Collins–Peter Holm divorce trial left her branded forever as the Passion Flower. She claimed she was the "other woman." She told a hushed courtroom that when she first had sex with Holm, he sprinkled rose petals on her body and said, "Now I want to smell the passion flower."

Danielson, who was usually identified in the press as a "buxom starlet," cemented her acting reputation with a performance that is etched in the minds of those at the trial: she fainted on the stand during her testimony.

Holm, who was usually identified in the press as a "former Swedish pop singer," didn't get what he asked for in the divorce. (He requested $80,000 per month in support "in order that I can maintain my standard of living which I have enjoyed previous to and during our marriage.") But he did make off with $180,000 and a $40,000 custom-made car. Not bad for a few months' work.

☆ **Getting There:** The Holm-Collins home where Peter and Passion Flower would rendezvous while Joan was at work on the set of "Dynasty" was at 1196 Cabrillo Dr. in Beverly Hills. Peter and Joan bought it together for $1.95 million. He didn't even bother to ask for it in the divorce settlement, bemoaning, "I realize that to live in a property like the Cabrillo residence may be unrealistic for me at this time." Or ever, Pete. From Sunset Blvd. take Coldwater Canyon Dr. north. Cabrillo Dr. turns off to the left.

THE SWEET SWING

He is arguably the best hitter in baseball: a lifetime average of .356, winner of five batting titles, seven consecutive seasons with two hundred or more hits, the latter something neither Ty Cobb nor Pete Rose ever accomplished.

But baseball hero Wade Boggs was revealed to have cleats of clay when mortgage banker Margo Adams went public with the story of their four-year affair.

They met on April 2, 1984, at a bar in Anaheim called Crackers. They went out with another couple for dessert, pastry dessert, not what you're thinking. It was all on the up and up, until their first date.

That first date they went for dinner to the Ancient Mariner in Newport Beach, California. That was when Boggs explained his theory of hitting. "There are hits in chicken," Margo quoted him as saying.

Margo later sued Boggs, claiming he broke a contract to pay her for lost wages and services during their four-year affair.

☆ **Getting There:** The Ancient Mariner is at 2607 West Pacific Coast Highway in Newport Beach. There are hits, among other things, in its chicken. The phone number is (714) 646-0201. From the airport (LAX), take Century Blvd. to I-405 south. Take 405 south all the way to Newport Beach (it's about 45 miles). Exit onto the 55 freeway and go south (still heading toward Newport Beach) until it turns into Newport Blvd.; stay on that until you see signs for the Pacific Coast Highway. Take the Pacific Coast Highway south toward San Diego; the Ancient Mariner will be a quarter of a mile down on the right-hand side (the water side).

CONGRESS AT CONGRESS

What made Congressman John Jenrette famous wasn't his participation in ABSCAM nor his later shoplifting charge. It was the admission by his wife, bombshell Rita Jenrette, that she and John had made it on the steps of the Capitol once.

☆ **Getting There:** The G-Spot, where John and Rita had their own little congress, is on the east side of the Capitol in Washington, D.C.

NOT A DOLLY PARTON JOKE

In his unpublished memoir *Hey Porter*, which was serialized in a tabloid, Porter Wagoner claimed to have nailed Dolly Parton the first time in the Magnolia Motel in Hammond, Louisiana, but Dolly didn't confirm it.

☆ **Getting There:** The Magnolia Motel is at 1111 Thomas St. The phone number is (504) 345-3196. From 55 south, take Exit 31 (Highway 190) to Hammond. Take a right at that exit (you'll be going west on 190); the motel is about one and three-quarters miles from there.

NOT A PORTER WAGONER JOKE

Porter also claimed to have bedded Tammy Wynette at the Anchor Motel in Nashville. Tammy claims he did not.

☆ **Getting There:** The Anchor Motel was at 1921 West End Ave. in Nashville. It closed in 1976.

BEFORE THOSE CRAZY RUMORS ABOUT ROCK HUDSON AND JIM NABORS...

I don't know what went on inside the apartment on Sweetzer Avenue. All I know is that Cary Grant invited Randolph Scott to move in with him, Scott accepted, and the studio wasn't happy at all.

But Cary and Randy were. You can see the happiness in their faces in poolside snapshots made at the house.

☆ **Getting There:** Cary Grant and Randolph Scott lived at 1129½ North Sweetzer Ave. in West Hollywood in 1932. Go west on Santa Monica Blvd. Six blocks past Fairfax is Sweetzer. Turn right.

They then moved to 2177 West Live Oak Dr. in the summer. From Santa Monica Blvd. take Western Ave. north until it turns right and becomes Los Feliz Blvd. Turn left on Fern Dell Rd. Go left on Black Oak to Live Oak East and left on it to West Live Oak. Turn right.

Even after Grant married Virginia Cherill, in 1934, he and Randy remained close, as in next-door neighbors at LaRonda Apartments on Havenhurst. Mr. and Mrs. Grant were in Apt. 10. Scott was next door in Apt. 11. Grant and Cherill were divorced less than a year later, and Cary and

Randy lived together at 1038 Palisades Beach Rd. (also called Pacific Coast Highway). It's just down the road from the JFK-MM sin den. See page 75 for directions.

LIZ TAYLOR AND CHICKEN

It was a dangerous pair from the word go: Liz Taylor at her peak (weight-wise) and a mess of fried chicken.

She was on the rubber chicken circuit with then-husband John Warner, who was running for the Senate seat in Virginia. In the process of devouring the food, Liz started choking. Liz was turning blue. Diners were alarmed. Help was summoned. Heimlich was performed. Liz was all right.

The event was later spoofed on "Saturday Night Live" with John Belushi playing Liz as a disgusting slob.

☆ **Getting There:** It was at the Bonanza Steak House at 506 East Gilley St. in Big Stone Gap, Virginia. From Abingdon, Virginia, take I-81 to US 23. Once you're on US 23, you'll see signs directing you to Bonanza.

THE DEVIL AND FIRST NORTH AMERICAN SERIAL RIGHTS

It was a dangerous liaison: the devil and a fourteen-year-old boy. The Catholic Church was called in to exorcise the demon. The resultant incident in Mount Rainier, Maryland, would form the basis for the movie *The Exorcist*.

It started January 18, 1949, when strange shrieks were heard coming from the home at 3210 Bunker Hill Road. Furniture and other household objects were clattering around unaided. Father Albert Hughes of nearby St. James Catholic Church was sent in to exorcise the demon. Father Hughes was injured during the four-month exorcism when the boy tore lose his leather manacles, sending a bed spring at the priest. It slashed the father's left arm, leaving a permanent scar.

The exorcism was unsuccessful, and the boy was sent

"The Exorcist" vacant lot.

to Alexian Brothers Hospital in St. Louis, where a Jesuit priest was able to exorcise the demon.

☆ **Getting There:** Take US 1 north from Washington, D.C. Go left on SR 501 to Mount Rainier. The house on Bunker Hill Road has been torn down.

　　To get to Alexian Brothers: From I-55 take Exit 204 and follow the signs. It's on Broadway. The wing where the exorcism took place has been torn down.

CLARA AND USC

One of the great legends of Hollywood is the story of the night in 1927 when actress Clara Bow, the It Girl, *entertained* the entire University of Southern California football team. The *entire* team, including a little-known lineman named Marion Morrison. Morrison would become an actor and change his name to John Wayne. Yes, that John Wayne.

☆ **Getting There:** Bow's home at 512 North Bedford was the scene of the orgy. From Santa Monica Blvd. in Beverly Hills take Bedford north one-half block.

FAMOUS FOR BEING FAMOUS

―――

Author James Monaco defines *celebrity* as someone well-known for their well-known-ness. In other words they are famous for being famous.

And we all want to get close to fame.

You can actually get close enough to celebrity to smell its bad breath. Maybe even walk in its footsteps. This chapter tells you how.

FAMOUS FOR CELEBRITY WEDDINGS

Getting hitched? Why not do it where the stars do, in Vegas? No waiting period. No blood test. Hey, they'll even pick you up and take you to the marriage license bureau if you want. And they accept out-of-state checks.

So the only decision to make is: where? You have a choice of forty-one commercial wedding chapels. But really only a half dozen cater to the stars.

The most famous is **Little Church of the West.** It's been around since 1942. Fernando Lamas and Arlene Dahl were wed there in 1954. David Cassidy and Kay Lenz pledged their eternal love there in 1977. And more recently Steven Adler, drummer for the hard-rock group Guns N' Roses, married longtime live-in love Cheryl Lynn Swiderski there. The *National Inquirer* reported Adler agreed to the marriage only after Swiderski agreed to let him continue having all the affairs he wanted.

☆ **Getting There:** Little Church of the West is at 3960 Las Vegas Blvd. South (The Strip!), just south of the Hacienda Hotel. Go to the Strip—you'll recognize it immediately; it's the only place in America where wanting to see Wayne Newton perform seems normal.

Other celebrity wedding mills:

- Melanie Griffith and Don Johnson were married the first time at the **Silver Bell Wedding Chapel.** She was eighteen and he was twenty-six. Their cabdriver was the witness. It's at 607 Las Vegas Blvd. South.

- Griffin O'Neal and hairdresser Rima Uranga were married the July Fourth weekend 1989 at the **Candlelight Wedding Chapel.** Ryan was there in a T-shirt. It *was* a formal T-shirt. Other stars who've gotten hitched there include Whoopi Goldberg, Bette Midler, Patty Duke, Barry White, John Byner, and Michael Caine. It's at 2855 Las Vegas Blvd. South, right next to El Rancho and across from Circus Circus.

- Heavy-metal heartthrob Jon Bon Jovi married his high school sweetheart at the **Graceland Wedding Chapel** (not affiliated with Elvis). It was also the scene of Lorenzo Lamas's most recent marriage. It's at 619 Las Vegas Blvd. South. And *Se Hablas Español!*

- Mickey Rooney liked **Chapel of the Bells** so much he used it for three of his weddings. Ernest Borgnine was another customer. It's at 2233 Las Vegas Blvd. South.

- The **Little White Chapel** was the scene of only two of Mickey Rooney's weddings, and Patty Duke only *renewed* her vows there. But Joan Collins and Peter Holm were married there. And Bruce Willis and

Demi Moore selected the chapel to perform an in-room ceremony. It's at 1301 Las Vegas Blvd. South, a mile north of the Sahara Hotel.

The cost for a Vegas wedding begins at $45 and goes up. Quickly.

FAMOUS FOR BEING FORMERLY FAMOUS

That's Sonny Bono, former star, strolling out of the Palm Springs City Hall. He's the mayor. (And wouldn't that be a great idea for a sit-com?)

That's right: Sonny Bono is the mayor of Palm Springs, California. One of his more publicized initiatives since taking office was to trim the town's deficit by selling T-shirts bearing his own likeness.

☆ **Getting There:** The Palm Springs City Hall is on Mc-Callum Way at the airport. If you come in on Highway 111

Celebrity city hall.

follow the signs. Or take Farrell St. north from 111 and turn east on McCallum.

FAMOUS FOR *LEAN ON ME*

Joe Clark, principal of Eastside High School in Patterson, New Jersey, was the most famous school official in America. He roamed the halls of his school with a bullhorn and a ball bat; the one to make sure his words were heard, the other to make sure his words were obeyed. The movie *Lean on Me* was based on his tenure at Eastside. When he took over as principal in 1982, chaos reigned. Drug dealers roamed the halls, as did students who were supposed to be in class. No more.

He installed a little old-fashioned discipline. He had his detractors, to be sure. Some parents criticized him when he chained the school doors shut to keep out drug dealers. But Clark doesn't let it bother him. He says, "A person is just like a tea bag. To see how strong he is, you have to put him in hot water." (He has since left the school.)

☆ **Getting There:** From Newark, take the Garden State Parkway north to Exit 156 Route 20. Take Route 20 to the Market St. exit (which may also be marked "Patterson Exit"). Follow Market St. to Madison Ave.; take a right on Madison Ave. Go to the second right (where you'll see a Shell station on the corner); take a left onto Park Ave. The school is two blocks ahead on the left: 150 Park Ave.

FAMOUS FOR LENNON'S REMARKS

John Lennon was very depressed. His marriage was in trouble.

He was also very plastered when he and his drinking pals entered the Troubador nightclub in Los Angeles. In a drunken whimsy, he taped a Kotex to his forehead. And kept on drinking. And talking. And nagging. When the waitress refused to give him what he thought was proper respect, he snapped, "Don't you know who I am?" "Yeah," she responded. "You're some asshole with a Kotex on his head."

☆ **Getting There:** The Troubadour is at 9081 Santa Monica Blvd., near Doheny. It was also the scene of a Bette Midler flash (she dropped her blouse for a nanosecond).

FAMOUS FOR J. D. SALINGER'S LAST INTERVIEW

"What really knocks me out is a book that, when you're all done reading it, you wish the author that wrote it was a terrific friend of yours and you could call him up on the phone whenever you felt like it. That doesn't happen much, though."

Remember Holden Caulfield making that wish in the most famous of all coming-of-age novels, *The Catcher in the Rye*?

J. D. Salinger, the writer who penned those words some forty years ago, seems to take an opposing point of view when he is the author in question. Don't try to call him up. He is a recluse, and a churlish one at that. (Also, his phone number is unlisted.)

A free-lance writer and a photographer who tried to talk to him in 1988 got a shopping cart pushed their way.

The photographer, Paul Adao, told the *New York Post*, "He was hitting my hands. He said something like, 'Why don't you guys leave me alone?' "

☆ **Getting There:** Okay, so leave him alone! His last interview was in 1953. He was interviewed for the high school page of the *Claremont* (N.H.) *Daily Eagle*. The interview took place in a booth at Spa's in Windsor, Vermont. According to Robert Brown of Windsor, Spa's was right next door to Latches, a local theater. People would go to the movies and then stop at Spa's for coffee and a doughnut. Both are long gone. In their place is a park called the Constitution Common, which is two hundred feet south of the post office in downtown Windsor.

FAMOUS FOR SERVICE TO THE QUEENS

Arkansas plastic surgeon Dr. James Billie has, by his own admission, improved the physical appearance of 120 Miss America candidates over the years. He claimed 5 surgical patients among the 51 entrants in the 1989 pageant.

☆ **Getting There:** His office is at 10810 Executive Center Dr., Suite 201 in Little Rock, Arkansas. From Memphis, take Highway 40 west to I-30. Take I-30 west to 630. Take 630 west to Shackleford. Go left on Shackleford to Cloker, and take a right. Dr. Billie's office will be in the second building on the right. Cellulite removed and noses improved by appointment only.

FAMOUS FOR TATTOOS

Break up with Betty Lou? Get kicked out of the Avenging Angels? No longer speaking to Mother?

Want to get that tattoo celebrating Betty Lou or the Angels or Mother removed from your bicep? This is the place. This is where Mark Gastineau was going to have his 'Gitte tattoo removed. But then he and Brigitte Nielsen, his love—Sly Stallone's ex and the tall blonde in *Beverly Hills Cop II* that Eddie Murphy called "that big bitch"— got back together.

☆ **Getting There:** Dermatology Institute of Arizona is in Phoenix. Take I-17 south to Bell Rd. Take Bell Rd. east to Fortieth St. At the southeast corner of that intersection (of Fortieth St. and Bell Rd.) is the Desert Valley Medical Plaza; the institute is in Suite 125.

FAMOUS FOR CLIP JOBS

Don King has more memorable hair, but not by much.

So if you aren't quite ready for the Don 'Do, try the Al Bob, the style made famous by preacher-activist Al Sharpton.

☆ **Getting There:** Al Sharpton's hairdresser (he goes once a week at a cost of $100) is Primadonna Beauty Care at 616 Vanderbilt Ave. in Brooklyn.

If you'd prefer a haircut like that of fight promoter King (writer Rick Bozich once describing it as looking "like a man who just received his January heat bill"), you're out of luck. A spokeswoman at King's office says he doesn't get his hair cut. "It doesn't grow."

FAMOUS FOR GOING BACK TO HER ROOTS, SO TO SPEAK

In 1989 Kim Basinger, the blubber-lipped blonde beauty of *Batman* fame, bought the entire town of Braselton, Georgia. She told *Vanity Fair* magazine she didn't plan to live there. "I'm here to preserve these fields. These are the lawns where I'd walk with my boyfriends. These are the fields where I learned oral sex."

☆ **Getting There:** From I-95 northeast of Atlanta take Exit 49 (SR 53) south. There it is. Kim owns the whole town. And the fields around the town . . . well, that's the school system.

FAMOUS FOR HIS FATHER

Frank Sinatra, Jr., was kidnapped shortly before he was to perform at a Nevada nightclub on December 8, 1963, by kidnappers whose only interest, oddly in these political kidnapping days, was money.

The FBI paid a ransom of $240,000 to the three kidnappers, Barry Keenan, Joe Amsler, and John Irwin. Actually the ransom sack was $15 short because an FBI microfilm machine had chewed up three five-dollar bills while copying serial numbers.

Sinatra was released after three days in captivity. Three days later the kidnapping trio was captured.

One of the kidnappers told police they had waded

barefoot through the money and even played Monopoly with it.

All served their time and all are now out.

☆ **Getting There:** Sinatra was kidnapped from Room 417 at Harrah's South Lodge in Lake Tahoe, California. It is on Highway 50 at Stateline, Tahoe. Call (800) 648-3773 for reservations.

FAMOUS FOR DAVID LETTERMAN BAGGING IT

While other members of the senior class at Broad Ripple High School in Indianapolis were practicing football or attending Key Club meetings, David Letterman was bagging groceries at the Atlas supermarket.

☆ **Getting There:** From I-65 take the 29th-30th St. exit and go east on 29th; take it to College. Go north on College to the 5400 block; the supermarket is 5411 North College.

FAMOUS FOR MOMMIE DEADEST

The sound of "No wire hangers!" may still reverberate through the air of Joan Crawford's former residence.

☆ **Getting There:** The *Mommie Dearest* house, where Joan abused her adoptive children, is at 426 North Bristol Ave. in Brentwood. From Sunset Blvd. turn north on Bristol. It's four blocks on the right.

FAMOUS FOR THE MAN WITH NO NAME

Clint Eastwood is one of the owners of the Hog's Breath restaurant in Carmel, California. It achieved notoriety in 1988 when it was closed down temporarily for health violations.

☆ **Getting There:** The restaurant is on San Carlos between Fifth and Sixth streets. From San Francisco, go south on Highway 101 and take the second Carmel exit (Ocean

Ave.). Take a right onto Ocean Ave. At the third stop sign, take a right onto San Carlos. The restaurant is one and a half blocks ahead on the left.

FAMOUS FOR FALLING

When he bought his Northwest Airlines ticket on the evening before Thanksgiving Day, 1971, D. B. Cooper had no idea he was soon to be a legend. His creativity won him a spot in the hearts of antiestablishment types everywhere.

For D. B. Cooper was the first hijacker to take along a parachute. Somewhere over the mountains between Seattle and Reno, he took his $200,000 and parachuted into the darkness. He was never heard from again. Some think he died in the fall, or perhaps in the wilderness. Others think he is somewhere on the beaches of Mexico, smiling as he reads this little story.

☆ **Getting There:** At the time authorities thought he came down near the shores of Lake Merwin, Washington. There's a small airstrip in View, Washington, and locals heard a plane land and take off again from there that night. From I-205 take SR 503 east to Ariel and the lake and start looking for footprints.

In 1980 a small boy found a packet of 299 twenty-dollar bills that had been among those Northwest delivered to Cooper. They washed up on the shore of the Columbia River near Vancouver.

Hollywood took a shot at Cooper's story (they didn't pay him for the rights) in the disappointing comedy-drama *The Pursuit of D. B. Cooper*, now available at video stores everywhere.

FAMOUS FOR BEING A NERD

Ed Greer, the D. B. Cooper of high-tech, walked away from his engineering job at Hughes Aircraft in LA in 1981 and vanished. Every year his old co-workers would celebrate the man who escaped the gray flannel world with an

Ed Greer party. They would wear Ed Greer masks and buttons that read PUT DOWN YOUR BEER AND VOTE FOR ED GREER. He was a hero to nerds everywhere until he turned up seven years later in Houston with an unexciting story. He'd been working all along. He just ran away from what he thought was a bad marriage.

☆ **Getting There:** Hughes Aircraft is at 7200 Hughes Terrace in Los Angeles. The phone number is (213) 568-7200. Go north on Sepulveda Blvd. from the airport, and take the Lincoln Blvd. exit. Go north on Lincoln Blvd. for about three miles; Hughes will be on the right-hand side as you head down a hill.

FAMOUS FOR NOT UNDERSTANDING

When Ernesto Miranda kidnapped and raped an eighteen-year-old woman in 1963, little did he know he would be making legal history.

When he was arrested, he was not informed of his right to remain silent and so he didn't. He blurted out the entire story. Police later claimed the confession was voluntary, quoting Miranda as making his statement "with full knowledge of my legal rights, understanding any statement I make may be used against me." The Supreme Court later overturned Miranda's conviction, refusing to believe he used such perfect English in understanding his rights and such grade school syntax in confessing: "Seen a girl walking up the street stopped a little ahead of her got out of car walked towards her grabbed her by the arm and asked her to get in the car."

The resulting legal doctrine has helped countless TV cop shows fill out a half hour with endless readings of *Miranda* rights: "You have the right to remain silent, pal. If you give up that right, anything you say can and will be used against you. You have the right to an attorney. If you cannot afford one the court will provide one.'"

☆ **Getting There:** Miranda was arrested and interrogated, but not read his rights, at Old City Hall, 17 South Second

Avenue in Phoenix. From I-17 take the Seventh Ave. exit. Go right on Buckeye to Second Ave. The rape occurred at Sixteenth St. and Bethany Home.

SEE SEAN SPIT

When Sean Penn finally crossed the line, committing an act that got him sent to jail, it wasn't in a nightclub or in an airport. It was while on location filming a movie. He spit on an extra, then slugged him; the judge voided his probation; and Mr. Penn went to the slammer.

Normally Sean's spitting match would happen outside the prying eyes of the public. But this was location filming and you could have been there. I'm sure if you had known ahead of time, you would have been.

Now a Hollywood company can help you find where Penn or any of the stars are filming. Hollywood on Location sells daily packets of information about where the cameras are. And watching location filming is as easy as showing up. That's because location filming is a public event. As long as you stay behind the police lines, you can watch to your heart's content.

On the day I visited, Hollywood on Location offered a list of three dozen location shoots, including *Throw Mama from the Train*, starring Danny DeVito and Billy Crystal (Berth 74, LA harbor); Richard Pryor's movie *Moving* (filming on Saddleback Road in LA) and Sean Penn's movie *Colors* (unfortunately not the day he spat).

Much like this book, Hollywood on Location is a self-guided tour.

You buy the packet, which includes the list of locations, maps, and suggestions (for $20.25, tax included), you decide what to see, you provide the transportation. Your list tells you what will be happening at the site and during what time span, but there are no guarantees.

The main stars may not be there that day, the scenes may take place out of view, or the whole shebang could be canceled. Or you might find the location and spend hours waiting. That's the way filming goes.

Or you could get lucky and see Sean Penn spit on an extra.

☆ **Getting There:** Hollywood on Location is on the second floor at 8644 Wilshire Blvd., Beverly Hills. Because the number of packets on a given day is limited, you should call (213) 659-9165 for reservations. From I-10 take the La Cienega Blvd. exit. Go north to Wilshire Blvd., then turn left. It's between Carson Rd. and Willaman Dr. Hours are 9:30 A.M. to 5 P.M. weekdays.

CELEBRITY DIRT

If you want real celebrity dirt, throw away your *National Enquirer,* cancel your subscription to *People,* and turn off "Entertainment Tonight."

Call Barry Gibson. He has the real thing, dirt he dug from the lawns of Johnny Carson, Michael Jackson, Shirley MacLaine, and forty-three other celebrities.

He sells the dirt in vials via mail order and in novelty shops. It runs $1.95 a vial, 55 cents less than a copy of *People.*

You can call Gibson's business an underground operation. None of the stars know of these forays into their private terrain. Gibson says he used to send letters asking for permission to dig; all he would ever get back were autographed photographs. He only digs by day so that no one mistakes him for a robber.

☆ **Getting There:** The mailing address for Celebrity Dirt is Box 55981, East Side Station, Lansing, MI 48929.

STAR WEARS

Have you ever seen Charo guest-starring on the "$20,000 Pyramid" and thought to yourself, She looks awful in that leather skirt. That should be worn by someone younger, not as full-bodied. Like me.

Your wish is Susie Cuehlo's command.

Cuehlo, who is Sonny Bono's ex-wife (but isn't Cher), is co-owner of A Star Is Worn, a Los Angeles boutique that sells designer gowns, furs, jewelry, even casual wear from the closets of celebrities. Even Cher.

The store also sells items worn in films and television shows.

When I visited, the former Mrs. Bono was offering for sale:

- A strapless black velvet bra signed by Cher, for $575.
- A needlepoint flower that had been hand-stitched by "one of Elvis's aunts," for $3,500. It previously had hung in the game room of his Beverly Hills mansion.
- A handkerchief used—we hope only to wipe his brow —by Warren Cuccurullo of the rock group Duran Duran, for $25.
- A white leather cowboy jacket previously owned by Cathy Lee Crosby, for $1,400.
- Black boots formerly owned by dancer Tatiana Y. Thumbzen, the number-two girl in Michael Jackson's video "The Way You Make Me Feel," for $750.
- A pink knit dress from Rosanna Arquette, for $45.
- The tuxedo Michael Nouri wore in *Flashdance,* for $675.

Unless a garment is a signed collector's item, it's priced to move. A percentage of each sale goes to charity. To boot.

☆ **Getting There:** A Star Is Worn is at 7303 Melrose Ave. at Poinsetta Pl., just west of LaBrea. From the Hollywood Freeway take the Melrose Ave. exit west. To get on the store's mailing list and receive periodic mail order offers call (213) 939-4922.

LIFESTYLES OF THE RICH AND HOMELESS

—

Where's Robin Leach when you need him? Probably on some remote island screaming into the microphone about how lovely Morgan Fairchild always vacations at this exclusive getaway.

Robin, tell us about the real lifestyles of the rich and famous, about how they skip out on small debts and chintz with the help.

Tell us about the Helmsleys.

THE BIGGER THEY ARE, THE SMALLER THEY ARE

If you live in the New York area, you've seen Leona Helmsley, the self-styled "Hotel Queen of New York," in television commercials touting the hotels that she and her husband, Harry, own.

If you live outside New York, you probably saw her on "60 Minutes" or on the news during her much-publicized trial for income-tax evasion (she was convicted).

Leona and Harry aren't as famous as New York real

estate tycoon Donald Trump, but they are richer. They are New York City's largest property owners with holdings valued at $8 billion. They own seven hotels, twenty thousand apartments, and the Empire State Building.

Harry ranked eighteenth on the 1988 Forbes 400 list of the country's richest.

But you know the old story: the bigger they are, the smaller they are.

In July 1988 a Greenwich, Connecticut, contractor sued the Helmsleys, claiming they never paid him for painting the Helmsley mansion driveway red for Leona's birthday. Daniel F. MacNamee & Co. claimed the Helmsleys owed $31,022.

Earlier that same year the Helmsleys were charged on 188 state counts of tax fraud and falsifying business records and another 47 federal charges of tax evasion. They were accused of evading income taxes by charging off $4 million in renovations to that same mansion as business expenses. Leona was convicted on a number of the charges. Harry was ruled too sick to stand trial.

The renovations on the $11 million palace included enclosing one of the two swimming pools, adding a breakfast room with a marble dance floor on the roof, and purchasing a $45,000 clock—in the shape of the Helmsley Building on Park Avenue. Leona bought it for Harry for his birthday.

Joseph Licari, the Helmsley's one-time financial manager, told *Manhattan, inc.* magazine in 1987 that "[Leona] made me fire a whole department . . . right before Christmas in 1985."

The *New York Post* reported at the time of their tax indictment that they had recently left a trail of unpaid bills across the resort island of Barbados: a total of more than $9,000 for such items as security guards and dogs, rental cars, food, and phone calls.

☆ **Getting There:** The Helmsleys' Connecticut mansion, Dunnellen Hall, is at 521 Roundhill Rd. in Greenwich. All you can see is eight chimneys and a bit of red tile roof.

The Helmsley Palace, the crown jewel of the Helmsley Hotel chain, is at 455 Madison Ave. at Fiftieth St.

STOLEN PROPERTY

The Marcoses, Ferdinand and Imelda, were indicted in
1988 in federal court on racketeering charges, accused of
stealing $103 million from the Philippines to buy build-
ings in New York City.

If you'd like to see some of that property, here are
the sites of four buildings formerly owned by the Marcos
family.

☆ **Getting There:** They owned: the building at 200 Madison
Ave.; the Herald Center shopping mall at One Herald
Square, right near Macy's; the Crown Building, at 730
Fifth Ave.; 40 Wall St. at, well, 40 Wall St.

IMELDA MARCOS'S SHOE STORE

Imelda Marcos has become synonymous with shoes.
    To wit:

- When the *Calgary* (Canada) *Herald* reported that a
  closet full of shoes belonging to the wife of International Olympic Committee president Juan Antonio
  Samaranch had been found, the story quoted un-
  named maids and bellhops calling the shoes "a collection that rivals Imelda Marcos."

- When it was disclosed that Panamanian strongman
  Manuel Noriega had a collection of two hundred mil-
  itary caps, an aide said, "Caps are to Noriega what
  shoes were to Imelda Marcos."

- A 1987 *USA Today* story said, "Imelda Marcos could
  have used Neil Balter. He knows all about our old
  shoes."

- Another 1987 *USA Today* story said, "A New York
  man who called himself the 'Shoe Doctor' collected

$379,000 from Medicaid for 'orthopedic' footwear when what he really sold clients was sneakers. He and Imelda Marcos would have made a great pair."

- One CNN report on her appearance in court focused on the shoes she wore.

It became such a hot topic that Christie's East used the shoes to draw a crowd to a February 1988 auction of Marcos property.

Why the big deal over Imelda's shoes? Well, when opposition leaders went into the Malacanang Palace in the Philippines after the Marcoses fled the country, they found 1,200 pairs of Imelda's size 8½ shoes, including a pair of blinking disco shoes.

Why didn't anyone make a big deal over the ten grand pianos? Or the pastel murals of Ferdinand and Imelda portrayed as Adam and Eve?

Well, it's hard to ignore 1,200 pairs of shoes.

They bring to mind a number of questions. Why? Did she wear them all? And where did she get them?

We answer only the last question.

Imelda Marcos's shoe store.

☆ **Getting There:** She bought many of them at Susan Bennis Warren Edwards, a chichi Manhattan store. Susan Bennis Warren Edwards is at 440 Park Ave.

TAMMY BAKKER'S SHOP-'TIL-YOU-DROP WORKOUT

In April 1987 Tammy Faye Bakker was seen trying on a tiger-print miniskirt with ruffles at the Palm Desert Town Center shopping area near Palm Springs, California.

☆ **Getting There:** The Palm Desert Town Center is at 72840 Highway 111, Palm Desert, California. Take Highway 10 east from LA. Go past Palm Springs. Exit onto Monterey Ave.; turn right. Take Monterey Ave. to Highway 111; the shopping center will be on the corner.

MORE SHOP-'TIL-YOU-DROP SIGHTINGS

An unidentified Oldham County, Kentucky, woman told Kit Millay, editor of the *Oldham Era*, that she spotted Tammy Faye Bakker shopping at My Three Sisters boutique in Daytona Beach, Florida, in the summer of 1989.

☆ **Getting There:** It is at 2563 North Atlantic Ave., in the Bellair Plaza Shopping Center. Atlantic Ave. is the strip where all the big hotels are; the boutique is across the street from the ocean and the plaza.

SHOP 'TIL YOU DROP, PART THREE

Another professional shopper is Michele Duvalier, wife of deposed Haitian dictator Jean-Claude "Baby Doc" Duvalier. During one binge she dropped $1.7 million at Saks, Cartier, and Susan Bennis Warren Edwards.

☆ **Getting There:** Saks is at Fifth Ave. and Forty-ninth St. Cartier is at 653 Fifth Ave. at Fifty-second St. Susan Bennis Warren Edwards is at 440 Park Ave.

LIVE-BEAT

You know Sheik Mohammed al-Fassi. Or at least you know of him.

He was the obscenely wealthy Saudi Arabian prince who caused such a stir when he purchased a mansion on Sunset Boulevard, the main thoroughfare of that chichi village, and had his yard men paint the genitalia hair on all the statuary on the front lawn. He took gauche to a higher plane.

He moved to Miami, bought an island, donated twenty grand to the tacky town of Opa Locka (in return they named a vacant lot Mohammed al-Fassi Park) and proceeded to run up $1.5 million in hotel bills for his entourage. He was thrown in jail when his checks to cover the bills bounced. But he was sprung after his lawyer pleaded that his money was tied up because of a foreign-exchange problem at a Swiss bank. He then ran up more bills at the Diplomat and then the Everglades before skipping out to Saudi Arabia.

☆ **Getting There:** His Florida mansion, which had $2.1 million in contractor liens on it, is on Star Island. From Miami take the MacArthur Causeway toward Miami Beach. Star Island is the second island on the left past Watson Park.

The Diplomat hotel is at 3515 South Ocean Dr. in Hollywood, Florida. The Everglades Hotel, which he stuck for $28,000, is at 3002 Biscayne Blvd. The sheik and his friends had the top two floors.

STEAL THIS CHAPTER

——

It was a strange time in American history. The pampered children of the upper class somehow got it in their heads that they wanted revolution. They just had some funny ideas about how to achieve it.

PATTY HEARST

The pampered heiress and her nerd boyfriend were at home in their Berkeley, California, apartment the night of February 4, 1974, when two large, black males burst in, abducting Patty Hearst and knocking Steven Weed around a little bit. Soon everyone in the country knew about the SLA, the Symbionese Liberation Army, a radical group that wanted to feed the poor and collect a few million from the Hearst newspaper family.

It was like a bad soap opera. The SLA would issue demands, Patty's parents would cry and give a little food to the poor, and the SLA would say it wasn't enough, and issue more demands.

The strangest twist came two months later, when Patty announced that she was no longer the poor, kidnapped heiress but had joined her captors in their revolutionary project. She was TANIA! On April 15 she showed up on a bank camera's film, participating in the robbery of the Hibernia Bank.

The end for the SLA came in a shoot-out with Los Angeles police. Six SLA members died when their safe house burned to the ground.

Hearst was captured September 18, 1975, in San Francisco. She later spent some time in jail for her part in the Hibernia robbery and is now a Connecticut housewife. She recently took time out from homemaking to play David Nelson's wife in the movie *Cry Baby.*

☆ **Getting There:** Patty and Steven lived in Apt. 4 at 2603 Benvenue. It's near the University of California–Berkeley campus. Get to the university. Take Shattuck Ave. south to Dwight Way, take it east to Benvenue, and head south.

The Hibernia Bank is on the northeast corner of Noriega and Twenty-second St. in San Francisco.

The SLA's final shoot-out was at 1466 Fifty-fourth St., in Los Angeles. From the Harbor Freeway, take Slauson Ave. east to Avalon. Go north five blocks to Fifty-fourth. Turn left on Fifty-fourth. Halfway down the street is the vacant lot where 1466 stood.

Patty was captured in the second-floor apartment at 625 Morse Ave. in San Francisco.

She served her time in the women's prison in Pleasanton, California.

CHICAGO 8, JUDICIAL SYSTEM 0

It was stranger than "Gilligan's Island." One of the defendants was bound and gagged and tied in his chair. Another wanted to kiss the jurors. It was the trial of the so-called Chicago 8. The eight professed radicals were charged with assorted crimes—rioting, etc.—during the Democratic National Convention. Sure that they couldn't receive justice in the courtroom of ancient Judge Julius Hoffman, the eight tried to turn the trial into a circus. And succeeded. Eventually Bobby Seale's indictment was severed from the case and they became the Chicago 7.

☆ **Getting There:** Abbie Hoffman, Jerry Rubin, Tom Hayden, David Dellinger, Rennie Davis, Lee Winer, John Froines, and Bobby Seale were tried in the courtroom on the twenty-third floor of the Federal Building in Chicago. The building is on Dearborn between Adams and Jackson.

WEATHERMAN EXPLOSION

The most radical of the student revolutionary groups of the sixties—remember the sixties?—was SDS, Students for a Democratic Society. And the most radical element of SDS was the Weather Underground, the Weathermen, a group that took its name from a line in a Bob Dylan song. (Did you know Bob Dylan now performs at state fairs and in Atlantic City casinos?)

And for all the group's posturing about changing the country, about the only visible change they made was to the Greenwich Village landscape.

On March 6, 1970, Weatherman Terry Robbins accidentally short-circuited the bomb he was assembling in a town house there. The resulting explosion killed him and two others, Diana Oughton and Ted Gold, and completely demolished the quarter-million-dollar town house, which belonged to radical Cathy Wilkerson's father.

Wilkerson and Kathy Boudin, who were also in the house at the time, staggered half naked into the street. They were taken in by Henry Fonda's ex-wife Shirley, who had no idea who they were or what they had been up to. She took them to her nearby apartment, gave them clothes, and let them use her shower. They left without thanking her.

☆ **Getting There:** The town house in Manhattan was at 18 West 11th St.

FOUND UNDERGROUND

Bernadine Dohrn was more famous at the time, but over the years the title of most famous female fugitive of the sixties student movement fell to Weather Underground member Kathy Boudin, who lived underground for more than a decade before she was finally captured after a bank robbery.

Until her final capture, which came after a botched armored car robbery, Boudin was wanted for only minor offenses, many of which had already been dismissed. But two cops and a security guard were killed during that heist, and she took a big fall.

For three years of her fugitive period she lived in Manhattan with Rita Jensen, a reporter for the *Paterson* (New Jersey) *News*. It wasn't until the end that Jensen discovered the true identity of the woman she knew as Lynn Adams, a waitress from Denver.

☆ **Getting There:** Boudin and Jensen shared a sixth-floor apartment at 50 Morningside Dr. in Manhattan.

Boudin was finally captured at a police roadblock on the eastbound ramp of interchange 11 of the NY Thruway. She and her accomplices had just robbed an armored truck at the nearby Nanuet Mall and switched cars at the Korvette Shopping Center. She eventually pleaded guilty to one count of murder and one count of armed robbery, and in 1984 was sentenced to twenty years to life.

DRY OUTS

You don't have to clean up your act by yourself anymore. You just pay someone else to do it for you. Then if it doesn't work—hey, it's their fault, not yours. Here are where the rich and famous go to dry out.

THE BETTY FORD CENTER

This is the place you've read about in every publication from *National Lampoon* to *National Enquirer*. It was even referred to in Lily Tomlin's Broadway show, *The Search for Signs of Intelligent Life in the Universe.*

This is where the rich and famous come to dry out.

Who knows who might be here today. You can park in the nearby Eisenhower Medical Center lot and watch the porch. Who's that coming out for a relaxing, drug-free sunning? Is it Liz or Mary Tyler Moore on a return visit? Or maybe one of the other celebrities who have cleaned up here: Tammy Bakker or Tammy Wynette, Stevie Nicks or

Betty Ford Center: celebrity dry out haven.

Tanya Tucker, or maybe Johnny Cash, Liza Minnelli, Chevy Chase, Tony Curtis, or Jerry Lee Lewis.

It costs $6,200 for a thirty-day stay and there is a one-month waiting list.

At the Betty Ford Center every patient is assigned a therapeutic duty, which may include such menial tasks as dusting or vacuuming. Maybe you'll get lucky and catch a glimpse of Liz Taylor taking out the trash. Right.

☆ **Getting There:** The address is 39000 Bob Hope Dr. in Rancho Mirage near Palm Springs, California. Take the Palm Desert exit from I-10 into Palm Desert, then west on SR 111 to Rancho Mirage. The Betty Ford Center is on the campus of the Eisenhower Medical Center and has its own set of buildings.

They don't really want tourists. So don't cause a scene. But you can sneak a peek by driving to the back of the Thomas Bannan Building. You can see over to the center through gaps in the bushes.

HAZELDEN REHABILITATION CENTER

Number two for celebrity dry outs is this respected treatment center located in Center City, Minnesota. It's been treating alcoholic and drug-dependent persons since 1949 and is generally recognized as the standard by which all other centers are measured.

In fact, Hazelden may soon be the star dry-out center of choice. It's a long ways from LA and all the media coverage, making it easier to sneak in and out.

Hazelden alums include designer Calvin Klein, TV star Sharon Gless, former pro basketball player Micheal Ray Richardson, pro football players Dexter Manley, Tommy Kramer, and Issiac Holt, actress Melanie Griffith, actor Howard Rollins, Jr., dancer Ben Vereen, and political spouse Kitty Dukakis.

Hazelden, like the Betty Ford Center, uses the Alcoholics Anonymous Twelve-Step-Program, mixed with the philosophies of the medical community and mental health practitioners. The cost is about $4,500 for a twenty-eight-day stay. Believe it or not, the costs at Hazelden and Betty Ford are low compared to many rehab centers.

☆ **Getting There:** Hazelden is about thirty miles northeast of Minneapolis, at 15245 Pleasant Valley Rd., Center City. From downtown Minneapolis, take 35 north for about thirty miles. Exit Highway 8 at Taylor Falls, and go east for about fourteen miles. Turn right on Pleasant Valley Rd. (about one mile past Center City), and two hundred yards later turn right again into Hazelden's driveway.

OTHER DRY-OUT CENTERS OF THE RICH AND FAMOUS

Betty Ford, whose very name is synonymous with drying out, actually went through alcohol detoxification and intervention at Long Beach Naval Hospital at 1720 Termino Avenue in Long Beach, California, south of Los Angeles, in 1978. It wasn't until October 1982 that the Betty Ford

Center in Rancho Mirage was dedicated by then vice president George Bush.

Kitty Dukakis spent her return engagement in treatment at the Edgehill Newport facility at 200 Harrison Avenue in Newport, Rhode Island.

Drew Barrymore, famous forever as the little sister in *E.T.*, couldn't handle the pressures of childhood stardom and entered the ASAP Family Treatment program at Van Nuys Hospital (15220 Vanowen Avenue.) in Van Nuys, California, in 1988 at age thirteen. At age fourteen she has written her autobiography.

Country star **George Jones** spent a month in 1987 recovering from "exhaustion" at University Hospital, 619 South 19th St. in Birmingham, Alabama.

Loretta Lynn, the coal miner's singing daughter, went through drug rehab for Librium addiction at Parkview Hospital, 230 Twenty-fifth Avenue N in Nashville.

Merle Travis was locked up at the Camarillo State Mental Hospital, 3998 Somis Road in Camarillo, California, for three months for his pill addiction.

Larry Gatlin and fellow Gatlin Brother **Rudy** kicked their cocaine habits at CareUnit Rehabilitation Center in Orange, California.

NUTS TO YOU

—

Maybe you've seen this bumper sticker: SUPPORT MENTAL HEALTH OR I'LL KILL YOU. This chapter studies the deeper meaning behind that bumper sticker.

SHOCKING REVELATIONS

Revelations that he had spent some time in the cuckoo closet cost Thomas Eagleton a chance at being the vice presidential candidate on the 1972 Democratic ticket, the one that made the party's worst showing ever in a presidential election. George McGovern and Sargent Shriver, Eagleton's replacement and Maria's father, were defeated almost two-to-one by Richard Nixon and Spiro Agnew.

☆ **Getting There:** Thomas Eagleton received treatment, including electroshock therapy, at Barnes Hospital in St. Louis in 1960. It's at 4949 Barnes Hospital Plaza. From I-40 take Kings Highway north. It's just a couple of blocks; it's on the right just before you get to the railroad tracks.

He also received treatment at the Mayo Clinic, in Rochester, Minnesota, in 1966. Take US 63 north to Rochester. It becomes Broadway. Go left on Second St. SW. It's right there.

IN MY ROOM

He was the most talented of the Beach Boys, also the tallest. But for some reason Brian Wilson was tormented by demons. He quit touring with the group in 1967 and quit everything in 1971, locking himself away in his Malibu mansion with his piano in a sandbox. His shrink was, and is, psychologist Dr. Eugene Landy, whose clients have also included Alice Cooper, Rod Steiger, and Weight Watchers founder Jean Nidetch. In early 1989 Landy was found guilty of one charge of improperly prescribing medication for Brian and surrendered his license to practice psychology for two years. The effect of the penalty was negligible. He continued as Brian's guru and began a new career as Brian's co-writer.

☆ **Getting There:** Dr. Eugene Landy's office was at 1516 Westwood Blvd. in Westwood, California. Landy earned a reported $50,000 a month treating Wilson. From the San Diego Freeway (I-405) go east on Wilshire Blvd. to Westwood. Go south on Westwood.

YOU TALKING TO ME

John Hinckley, the guy who took potshots at President Reagan on a D.C. street, pleaded insanity and is currently serving his time at St. Elizabeth Hospital in Washington, D.C. He was turned down for a work-release program in 1988 after Secret Service agents found a copy of a letter he sent to a mail order house to obtain a nude drawing of Jodie Foster. (Don't ask for the address of a mail-order firm trafficking in nude drawings of celebrities. That isn't in the scope of this book.)

☆ **Getting There:** St. Elizabeth Hospital is at 2700 Martin Luther King, Jr., Ave. SE. From the Anacosta Freeway take MLK Ave. north.

PSYCHO

The folks around Plainfield, Wisconsin, just thought Ed Gein was a mama's boy. Until that day in 1957 when police went to his farmhouse and found masks made of human faces, upholstery made of human flesh, and trash cans made of human bones and skin. There were human skulls on the bedposts, a human heart in the saucepan, and a belt made of female nipples in the drawer. And out in the summer kitchen was the eviscerated body of his most recent victim, decapitated and dressed out like a deer.

Ed Gein, fifty-one, a hermit and bachelor, was a sick young 'un. He openly told investigators about his expeditions to local cemeteries to rob graves. He had opened the graves of a Mrs. Sherman, a Mrs. Everson, a Mrs. Adams, a Mrs. Bergstrom, a Mrs. Evans, and a Mrs. Sparks at the Plainfield cemetery, where Gein's mother was also buried. He had disturbed the grave of a Mrs. Foster in the Hancock cemetery and a Mrs. Beggs from the Spiritland cemetery. He also committed at least one murder.

The Ed Gein story has been the basis of three movies: *Psycho, Texas Chainsaw Massacre,* and *Deranged* (which is the closest to the true story).

How do you pronounce Ed's last name? He told reporters at his 1968 trial, "Some people say 'Gine' but we —I—always said 'Geen.' "

Rhymes with fiend.

☆ **Getting There:** The Gein farmhouse was burned to the ground on March 27, 1957, shortly after word got out that someone planned to open it up as a tourist attraction called The House of Horrors. From Milwaukee, take 51 north to Highway 73 and the Plainfield interchange. Make a left at the bottom of the ramp. Go west on 73 to County Junction KK; make a left. When you come to the first crossroads, take a right; site of the farmhouse is one and a half miles later.

Gein was committed to Central State Hospital in Waupun, Wisconsin, a maximum-security institution for the criminally insane. It is now the Dodge Correctional Institute. It is at One West Lincoln St. in Waupun. From Milwaukee, take 41 north toward Green Bay. Take a left at Highway 49 (you'll see a Wickes Lumber), and go fifteen miles to Waupun. Once in town, take a left on Madison, and proceed past the main prison about two blocks. Turn right on Lincoln, go over the railroad tracks, and the Dodge Institute will be ahead on the left. Ed's dead.

THE ORIGINAL CUCKOO'S NEST

Ken Kesey worked and gathered material for *One Flew over the Cuckoo's Nest* at Menlo Park VA Hospital near San Francisco.

☆ **Getting There:** The hospital is at 3801 Miranda Ave. in Palo Alto, California. From the Golden Gate Bridge, go south on 101 to the Oregon Expressway. Go west on Oregon to the Foothill Expressway, and take a left. Stay in the left-hand lane. Take a left at Hillview and then an immediate right on Miranda.

NUTTIEST

It is the Betty Ford Center of nuthouses. Many of America's most famous fruitcakes served their terms in Bellevue Hospital, New York City. In *Miracle on 34th Street* Kris Kringle was sent to Bellevue for observation. Ray Milland's character in *The Lost Weekend* spent time in Bellevue's detox unit.

☆ **Getting There:** Bellevue Hospital is on First Ave. from Twenty-fifth to Thirtieth streets.

THE LEGEND OF ZELDA

After her crack-up, Zelda Fitzgerald, wife of author F. Scott Fitzgerald and writer in her own right, was institutionalized in Highland Hospital in Asheville, North Carolina, where she died in a fire in 1948.

☆ **Getting There:** The hospital is at 49 Zillicoa St. in Asheville. From Winston-Salem, take 40 west to 240 west to the Montford exit. Go right on Montford for about four blocks, and you will see signs for the hospital.

AVOID THE NOID

Kenneth Laram Noid finally had had enough of it, all the taunts, all the remarks. So in 1989 he took the law into his own hands, stormed the Domino's Pizza, and held employees at gunpoint. He was convinced he was the target of the Domino's Avoid the Noid advertising campaign. He forced his hostages to prepare him a pizza and then watch him eat it. He was later found not guilty of robbery and kidnapping by reason of insanity.

☆ **Getting There:** The Domino's Pizza that was attacked by the Noid is at 4763 Buford Highway, Chamblee, Georgia. If you're coming into Atlanta on I-75, take 285 east to Augusta-Greenville. About ten miles later, exit (left) on Buford Highway; Domino's will be about three miles ahead on the left.

THE VOLTAGE ALSO RISES

For the kids in our audience, Ernest Hemingway wasn't the inventor of the Bad Hemingway contest, held every year to recognize overstimulated prose. He actually invented the style the contest parodies and used it in a couple of books or so: *The Snows of Kilimanjaro, The Old Man and the Sea,* and a few others. He was depressed long before people were making fun of his style and in 1961 had electric shock treatments at the Mayo Clinic for his depression.

☆ **Getting There:** The Mayo Clinic is in Rochester, Minnesota. See page 111 for directions.

FRUITS OR NUTS?

When evangelist Jim Bakker cracked during his trial on charges of fraud and conspiracy, he was taken to the Federal Correctional Facility, a minimum-security prison, in Butner, North Carolina, for psychiatric evaluation. Other celebrities who spent time at Butner for evaluation were John Hinckley, the guy who shot President Reagan, and *Hustler* magazine owner Larry Flynt.

☆ **Getting There:** Butner Federal Correctional Facility is just off old Highway 75 in Butner. Once you get to Butner, anyone can tell you where the prison is.

Other celebrity nuthouses:

- Country singer **George Jones** was admitted to Hill Crest hospital in Birmingham, Alabama, in December 1979 following an onstage Donald Duck impersonation. It is at 6869 Fifth Ave. South. From I-65 south take I-20 east (past the airport), and exit on First Ave. north. Take that all the way past the airport and make a right on Sixty-eighth St. Go up the hill (through two signs and one light); take a left at the fork in the road where Sixty-eighth St. ends. The hospital is right at that corner.

- Actress **Frances Farmer** was hospitalized at the Western State Mental Hospital in Steilacoom, Washington, in 1944. From Tacoma, take I-5 south to Exit 129. Take the left-hand fork of Exit 129; take a left onto Sprague. Take Sprague to Eighty-fourth St., where you will make a right. Take a left on South Tacoma Way. One block later, turn right on Steilacoom Blvd.

Past Alberton's you will start to see signs for the hospital, which is across from a park.

And one emotional outburst . . .

WHERE ED MUSKIE CRIED AWAY THE PRESIDENCY

He was widely recognized as a good and decent man. During the 1968 election many Democrats who opposed Hubert Humphrey's stance on Vietnam cut their bumper stickers in half, displaying only the MUSKIE side. So everyone just naturally assumed that Maine Senator Edmund Muskie would be the Democratic nominee for president in 1972. Then came New Hampshire.

Wounded by an attack on his wife, Jane, in the *Manchester Union Leader* (under the headline "Big Daddy's Jane," it repeated earlier news reports that she liked a predinner cocktail and that she had asked reporters if they knew any good dirty jokes), Muskie cried as he lashed out at the newspaper's publisher, William Loeb. With his tears went Ed Muskie's chance at the presidency.

☆ **Getting There:** Muskie cried, and the CBS News camera crew recorded it, on a flatbed truck in front of the offices of the Manchester Union Leader, at 35 Amherst St. in downtown Manchester, New Hampshire. From Nashua, go north on 93 and exit on the Granite St. Bridge (go right). Make a left on Elm; go through three lights and take a right on Amherst (about a block later).

BIRTHPLACES WE COULD DO WITHOUT

—

Most travel books take you to the birthplaces of long-dead patriots and goody-two-shoes movie stars. Who cares?

Wouldn't you rather see where something absolutely disgusting, like Howard Cosell, was born? So you can feel pity—and maybe a little superiority—toward the locals.

BIRTHPLACE OF GERALDO RIVERA

Geraldo Rivera, who began his TV career as plain old Gerry Rivers, may not be as despicable as the now-retired Howard Cosell, but he's all we've got.

Look on the bright side: he isn't a twin. At forty-six, the better part of his career is behind him.

☆ **Getting There:** Geraldo is circumspect about his origins. Perhaps he's afraid we'll learn his true age (he'll be forty-seven in July 1990). He was born in Williamsburg, New York. To get there cross the Williamsburg Bridge from Manhattan.

There's no "Welcome to Geraldo Rivera's Hometown" sign.

BIRTHPLACE OF LEGIONNAIRES' DISEASE

AIDS has a patient zero, but he's merely the one suspected of carrying the disease into this country. For most diseases no one knows where they started. Not so with Legionnaires' Disease. We know exactly where it started: at the Bellevue Stratford Hotel in Philadelphia during an American Legion convention in 1976. Twenty-nine conventioneers died from the soon-to-be-called Legionella bacteria.

☆ **Getting There:** Things got so bad for the Bellevue Stratford after it was linked to Legionnaires' Disease that the hotel had to change its name. It became the Fairmont. Now it is called the Hotel Atop the Bellevue. It is at Broad and Walnut streets, right in the center of the city. From I-95 take Lombard St. west eighteen blocks, then north seven blocks to Walnut. Call (215) 893-1776 for reservations.

BIRTHPLACE OF RICHARD NIXON'S POLITICAL CAREER

Before the Alger Hiss case, RMN was just a California congressman with a bad five o'clock shadow. His astute manipulation of the case against the accused spy landed him on the front pages of newspapers across America and was in large part responsible for his ascension to the Vice President's slot on the Eisenhower ticket in 1952. And the rest really is history.

The Hiss case is a complex one. In the forties Alger Hiss was a darling of the liberal intelligentsia—smart, handsome, well-connected. He was head of the Carnegie Endowment on International Peace and a former State Department employee. So when tubby, sexually uncertain Whittaker Chambers fingered him as a Commie spy, liberals were shocked. Conservatives leaped at the case. It was further proof that the State Department really was full of Commie spies.

Nixon ran point for the House Un-American Activities Committee in its investigation of Hiss. The turning point was when Chambers handed over what have come to be called the Pumpkin Papers. They were retyped State Department documents which Chambers said Hiss gave him to turn over to the Russians.

The documents, and several rolls of microfilmed government secrets, were called the Pumpkin Papers because Chambers hid them in a hollowed-out pumpkin in his garden.

☆ **Getting There:** Chambers's pumpkin patch was at his Westminster, Maryland, farm. From Westminster, Maryland, take Highway 97 north. Make a right on Bachman's

Whittaker Chambers's pumpkin patch.

Valley Rd. (State Route 496) and proceed east. When you get to the intersection of Bachman's Valley Rd. and Saw Mill Rd., look to the left and you'll see a big red barn; that's the farm.

BIRTHPLACE OF THE MALL

It all began here at the Country Club Plaza in Kansas City. It is the oldest shopping center in America, built in 1922. Thanks to the Country Club Plaza we now have a nation of climate-controlled malls, Spencer Gift Shops, Hickory Farms Cheese Shops, and Tiffany, the brat singer who got her start singing in malls.

☆ **Getting There:** Country Club Plaza is at 4629 Wornall Rd. in Kansas City, Missouri. From downtown Kansas City, take Main St. south to Forty-seventh St., and you'll see it.

BIRTHPLACE OF *HEAVEN'S GATE*

Was it only a coincidence that *Heaven's Gate* and Watergate both end in "gate?" Of course not. There are no coincidences in life.

Heaven's Gate has since become synonymous with "bad movie that cost millions."

The movie was director Michael Cimino's follow-up to his successful *Deer Hunter.* With success came arrogance and money, obscene amounts of money. *Heaven's Gate* ran way over budget and would have gone even more over budget if United Artists hadn't balked at a sweetheart deal Cimino had with himself—he bought 156 acres of Montana farmland and tried to charge the studio for improvements to use it for the battle scene. The movie ended up costing $44 million. (The initial budget was $11,588,000, so it went only $32,412,000 over budget.)

It opened November 18, 1980, and critics immediately pounced, calling the movie everything from "pretentious" (Canby, *New York Times*) to "ponderous spectacle" (Sarris, *Village Voice*). It was an unmitigated disaster, and the studio, United Artists, quickly pulled it from release. It is generally credited with bankrupting United Artists.

☆ **Getting There:** *Heaven's Gate* was filmed in Kalispell, Montana, near Glacier National Park. You'll have to get to Montana on your own. From I-90 at Missoula, it's 122 miles north. The cast and crew stayed at the Outlaw Inn on Highway 93. Production offices were on the top (fourth) floor. The town of Sweetwater was built in the parking lot on the edge of Two Medicine Lake in Glacier National Park. From Kalispell take US 2 to the south edge of the park.

BIRTHPLACE OF JUNK BONDS

Michael Milken didn't invent the junk bond. The high-yield, high-risk bonds had been around for years as a method of raising capital for small firms. What Milken did was convince the high-rollers that junk bonds could be used to fund takeovers and other big capital tasks. He effectively changed the way capital was allocated in this country.

But it all fell apart in December 1988 when the investment firm he worked for, Drexel Burnham Lambert, pleaded guilty to six felonies and paid a fine of $650 million.

In March 1989 Milken, his brother Lowell, and a third man were named in a ninety-two-count indictment, charged with racketeering, insider trading with Ivan Boesky, hiding stock ownership for a number of investors, defrauding investors of Fischbach Corporation, and a long list of other securities and mail frauds. The indictment asked for $1.8 billion in fines.

Milken is still fighting the charges at this writing, running up enormous legal fees. Of course in his last year at Drexel he reportedly was paid $500 million. That's for one year, folks. So he can probably afford enormous legal fees.

☆ **Getting There:** The offices of Drexel Burnham Lambert, Inc., are at 131 South Rodeo Dr., one block south of Wilshire Blvd. in a nondescript building in Beverly Hills.

BIRTHPLACE OF A STUPID FAD

We've seen a lot of fads come and go but none—NONE!—was worse than goldfish swallowing. There is nothing slimy or yucky about Hula Hoops or Frisbees, but who in his right mind would swallow a goldfish? The first was Harvard freshman Lothrop Withington, Jr., who probably did it to draw attention away from his stupid name. It was on March 3, 1939, after he had boasted to a friend that he had once done it. The friend didn't believe him. Ten-dollar bills were deposited on the table. And Withington did it again.

☆ **Getting There:** It was in a dorm room in Holworthy Hall at Harvard University, Cambridge, Massachusetts.

BIRTHPLACE OF THE COOKIE CUTTER COMMUNITY

If you think the developer who built your subdivision lacked imagination, you need to visit Levittown, New York. It was the original prefabricated suburbia. All the houses look exactly alike because they are exactly alike. In 1949 William Levitt turned a Long Island potato field into his vision of heaven: 17,447 ranch homes that looked like they had all come out of the same Play-Doh mold. For no money down and $60 a month, you got the basic model, four rooms, attic, washing machine, barbecue grill, twelve-and-a-half-inch TV, and all the potatoes you could dig up in your backyard. When it was completed in 1951, it was home to 82,000 people.

☆ **Getting There:** It's on Long Island. From the North Street Parkway take Wantagh St. south to the Levittown exit.

BIRTHPLACE OF TOP FORTY RADIO

One night in 1957 Todd Storz, owner of a chain of mid-western radio stations, was having drinks in an Omaha bar with his local station manager, Bill Stewart. As the night got blurrier, they noticed that the bar's patrons were playing the same forty songs on the jukebox over and over. Storz and Stewart, two capable barflies, hung around past closing, and were further astonished that the waitresses, who had been listening to the same tired forty songs all evening, played those same songs while they did their clean-up chores.

The light bulb clicked on and a radio format was born. Stewart went back to his station, KOWH, and transformed it into a Top Forty station. Soon Storz stations in Kansas City and New Orleans were playing only forty songs. In Texas station owner Gordon McLendon heard this new format and adapted it to his stations in Fort Worth and Louisville, Kentucky. (Louisville changed formats by playing "Purple People Eater" for twenty-four straight hours.)

Soon every town in America had a Top Forty station.

All playing the same forty songs.

☆ **Getting There:** KOWH-AM was in the Kilpatrick Building, at the corner of Fifteenth and Farnam in downtown Omaha.

BIRTHPLACE OF *DIRTY DANCING*

We can always thank the movie *Dirty Dancing* for reviving the moribund career of face-man Patrick Swayze, whose inept acting ability was laid bare for all to see in the mini-series "North and South." Thank you, *Dirty Dancing*.

Swayze used his newfound popularity to let his public know that he was more than a pretty face and a pretty body. "*Dirty Dancing* was a sweet little film, but I had a very specific point I wanted to bring off about class structure and social prejudice."

Yes, and that movie said it all. Thank you, *Dirty Danc-*

ing. And thank you, Patrick Swayze, for raising our consciousness level on class structure and social prejudice.

The movie not only resurrected Swayze's career and gave him a soapbox for his blitherings, it also gave us "Ride Like the Wind," the Patrick Swayze hit record, and "Swayze Dancing," the Patrick Swayze Learn-to-Dance video. *Dirty Dancing* wasn't born at an upstate New York summer resort, as you might have been led to believe, had you managed to follow the plot. It was actually filmed in southwestern Virginia.

☆ **Getting There:** The movie was filmed at the Mountain Lake Hotel in Giles County, Virginia, near the West Virginia border. From US 460 take SR 700. It is seven twisty miles. Just when you've given up hope of ever seeing another human being, there it is.

MISSPENT YOUTHS

T he town of Hunt, Illinois, is proud to call itself "Home of Burl Ives." Roanoke, Virginia, isn't ashamed to admit it is the childhood home of Wayne Newton. But Baltimore, Maryland, on the other hand, makes no mention on its welcoming sign of the birth there in 1949 of cross-dressing acting person Divine.

This misplacement of values is now corrected. Read on . . .

DIVINE: HER BOYHOOD HOME

Hollywood lost one of its biggest stars when Divine died on March 7, 1988. The female impersonator, who was born Harris Glenn Milstead in Baltimore, weighed close to 320 pounds at his/her death. Divine's manager, Bernard Jay, gave the cause of death as excessive weight.

Divine starred in seven "bad-taste" films by director John Waters, including *Pink Flamingos*, *Mondo Trasho*, and *Polyester*. His/her most famous performance was a dog-do-eating scene in *Pink Flamingos*.

Divine: her boyhood home.

Divine had seemed on the verge of mainstream stardom with the role of Edna Turnblad, the mother, in Waters's "good-taste" hit, *Hairspray*.

Divine's death site, a room in the Los Angeles Regency Plaza Hotel, is on the Grave Line Tour. (See Organized Scandal Tours, page 263.)

☆ **Getting There:** As a small child Divine lived in the apartment at 1824 Edgewood Rd. in Loch Raven, Maryland, just north of the Loch Raven Elementary School. Go south on Loch Raven Blvd. and turn left on Edgewood Rd. into Loch Raven Village Apts. Divine's parents no longer live there so don't stop for a chat. He also lived in the old Turnbull Estate on LaPaix Avenue in the Rodgers Forge area of Baltimore. It's since burned. It's where St. Joseph's Hospital is now.

CHARLES MANSON'S BOYHOOD HOME

You can read the Ashland, Kentucky, tourist brochure from cover to cover and not find any mention of its most famous former resident, Charles Manson.

The mass murderer, who is serving a life sentence in the Corcoran, California, prison (see Celebrity Hard Time, page 183) for masterminding the 1969 Tate-LaBianca murders, was born in Cincinnati to an unwed mother from Ashland who supported her baby by working as a prostitute. Because of his mother's erratic lifestyle, Charles Manson was often dumped at relatives' homes. A frequent residence was the home of his grandparents in Ashland.

Ward Harrison of Utica, Indiana, who occasionally corresponds with Manson, says Manson has written him that he can remember staying at his grandparents' Hilton Avenue home. They previously lived on East Central Avenue, but Harrison says Manson has no recollection of that house.

☆ **Getting There:** Manson's grandparents lived at 2105 Hilton. Take US 60 into Ashland. Near downtown turn right on Lexington Ave. Go up a block and turn right on Prospect, then left on the next street, which is Hilton. It's okay to drive by and gawk but don't stop and bother the folks who live there.

HOMETOWN OF COUNTRY MUSIC OUTLAW JERRY JEFF WALKER

Jerry Jeff Walker has the perfect name for country music. It sounds Texas. It sounds pickup truck. It sounds . . . perfect. Walker is famous for such country-rock ditties as "Up Against the Wall Red Neck Mother" and "Mr. Bojangles." He's also famous for some of his drinking bouts. The only thing that spoils it is when you find out his real name is Paul Crosby and he was born in Oneonta, New York, where the closest buffalo is Buffalo, New York.

☆ **Getting There:** The town is right on I-88 between Binghamton and Schenectady.

HOMETOWN OF BILLY THE KID

Although one of the many movies about cowboy legend William "Billy the Kid" Bonner is titled *The Kid from Texas*, the fact is Billy was not born in the Old West, or even close to the Old West. He was born in the Old East, in particular in New York City on the Upper East Side.

☆ **Getting There:** You can find New York City. It's on all the maps.

OTHER BOYHOOD HOMES

- Country music star **Merle Haggard**'s childhood homes included the Fred C. Nelles School for Boys in Whittier, California, and the Preston School of Industry in Ione, California, near Stockton.
- Rock pioneer **Chuck Berry** spent three of his formative years in the Algoa Intermediate Reformatory for Young Men (reform school) in Jefferson City, Missouri.
- **Steve McQueen** spent most of 1945 at Boys' Republic Reform School in Chino, California, for unruly behavior.

☆ **Getting There:** Fred C. Nelles School for Boys is in Whittier, California. From the San Gabriel River Freeway (I-605) take Whittier Blvd. east. The school is on the right at 11850 East Whittier Blvd. at the corner of Sorenson and Whittier. The Preston School of Industry is at 201 Waterman Rd. in Ione, California. Take 99 north to Twin Cities Rd. Go east on Twin Cities Rd., which is also Highway 104, all the way to the facility. You have to go approximately forty miles on Highway 104, and along the way you will pass Rancho Seco (a nuclear power plant with two big towers), the Amador County Line, the Mule Creek State Prison, and the Fire Academy. You'll know you're at the Preston School of Industry when you see the big castle; take a left.

Algoa Intermediate Reformatory for Young Men is near Jefferson City, Missouri. Take I-50 south about eight miles out of Jefferson City. When you see a highway patrol office on your left at the top of a hill, start looking for the Algoa Spur at the bottom of that hill. Take a left on the Algoa Spur; about three-quarters of a mile down you'll see the front gate across the railroad tracks.

Boys' Republic Reform School is now called Boys' Republic Rehabilitation Center. It is at 3493 Grand Ave. in Chino, California. Take I-60 south toward San Bernadino to the Corona (Highway 71) Expressway. Make a right at the Geary St. Exit and take that all the way to the Boys' Republic. (About a mile from where you turn, you'll make a quick right and then a quick left. Off to the right, you'll see a bunch of buildings and what looks like a farm—that's the Boys' Republic.)

LAND OF OPPORTUNITY

What a country!" Russian comedian Yakov Smirnov is fond of saying. Just ask these people, all of whom view this as the Land of Opportunity.

A BUSH IN THE HAND

Let's face it: George Bush didn't exactly grow up in a log cabin and walk two miles through the blinding snow to school. Texas official Jim Hightower put it succinctly when he said of President Bush's upbringing: "George Bush is a man who was born on third base and thinks he hit a triple."

Actually Bush was the first baseman on the Yale University baseball team, but he occasionally found himself on third base.

☆ **Getting There:** The Yale baseball stadium is in New Haven, Connecticut. From the Merritt and Wilbur-Cross parkways, take Exit 57 and Route 34 south (Derby Turnpike). Follow the turnpike directly to the bowl . . . or take Exit 59 (Whalley Ave.) and follow the Yale Bowl signs. From I-95, take Exit 44 and follow the Yale Bowl signs.

Third base is on the pitcher's right side as he faces the batter.

YOU WOULDN'T WANT TO DANCE, WOULD YOU?

The keynote speaker at the 1988 Democratic convention, Ann Richards, said of Bush: "What is it about George Bush that women don't like? It's very hard to explain unless you have ever gone to a high school dance . . . and see that guy that's constantly raising his eyebrows, and you say to yourself, Oh, Lord, I hope he doesn't ask me."

☆ **Getting There:** George Bush's high school was Philips Academy in Andover, Massachusetts. He graduated in 1942. According to school research, the prom in 1942 was held in the school gym on campus. It is off Salem St. I have no firm information on whether he raised his eyebrows and asked any young ladies to dance.

DAN QUAYLE'S DRAFT BOARD

Talk about someone for whom this is the Land of Opportunity: look no farther than Vice President Dan Quayle. Vice Presidents are historically the butt of jokes, but Dan has made it too easy.

Dan Quayle served his country during the Vietnam War by keeping the golf courses of north-central Indiana safe from Vietcong infiltrators. When he heard the word *draft,* Dan said, "Pour me another one."

Actually he said, "Daddy. I'm getting drafted." And daddy called a few of his influential friends in the Indiana National Guard and soon young Dan was protecting his country by typing for a quarterly magazine, the *Indiana National Guardsman.* His prose struck fear in the hearts of Vietcong journalists.

☆ **Getting There:** The draft board was in the post office building at 330 West Market in Huntington, Indiana. Market is the main downtown street. Huntington is six miles west of I-69 at the Highway 5 exit. Stay on Highway 5 and you'll run right into the courthouse. Go around the circle, over the railroad tracks, and make a left at Warren. Then take a left at Market and the post office will be three blocks down.

The National Guard Armory is at 800 Zahn in Huntington.

DAN QUAYLE'S FRATERNITY HOUSE

DePauw University in the sixties was, in writer Gail Sheehy's words, "a hotbed of social rest." And Dan Quayle was a major participant in that snoozing. He joined the Delta Kappa Epsilon fraternity, Dekes, at DePauw, and by his senior year he was president.

Dan Quayle's frat house. (Photo by Joe Whittaker)

It was at the Deke house that he studied "booze and broads," as his father put it in an interview. When asked about this, Dan's boss, George Bush, supposedly replied, "It's not just anybody who can carry a double major."

☆ **Getting There:** DePauw University is in Greencastle, Indiana. The Deke house is at 620 East Anderson. Take I-70 west from Indianapolis. Take Exit 41 (US 231) north. It's about six miles to the DePauw campus. Make a right at Anderson (it's a one-way street); the fraternity will be on the right side just past Delta Delta Delta and Alpha Omicron Pi. When you're facing the house, Quayle's room was on the third floor, middle of the house, right above the balcony. All three windows were his room; there were three to four guys to a three-room suite. Quayle slept in the room on the left.

THE DAN QUAYLE PRO-AM GOLF TOUR

Take it from Marilyn Quayle, who ought to know: Dan Quayle loves golf. It's been good to him. He was on a golf course when he got the word he was running for Congress. He was on a golf course when he got the word he would be running for Vice President.

In fact in 1986 he co-sponsored a bill that would give a tax break to visiting golf pros.

DAN'S FAVORITE GOLF COURSES

The Paradise Valley Country Club golf course in Phoenix, Arizona. Dan and family lived next to the eleventh tee from the time Dan was eight to sixteen. This is where he learned to play golf. He won a junior tournament here at twelve and made a hole in one at seventeen. By age eighteen he was a four-handicapper.

☆ **Getting There:** Paradise Valley is northeast of town. From I-17 take Exit 205 east to Paradise Valley. The club is at the corner of Lincoln Dr. and Tatum Blvd.

The Doral Country Club in Miami, Florida At the 1968 Republican convention in Miami Beach, Dan worked as a driver, escorting Nixon aides around the beach. He also played golf with them at the Doral Country Club.

☆ **Getting There:** From the Palmetto Expressway (SR 826) take NW Thirty-ninth St. west to NW Seventy-ninth St. Go right one block and left on NW Forty-first St. It takes you to the club.

The Norwood Golf Course in Huntington, Indiana He and Marilyn bought a home near the golf course.

☆ **Getting There:** The Norwood golf course is at 5961 West Maple Grove Rd. in Huntington, Indiana.

Other golf courses in Huntington:

- **LaFontaine Country Club** is at 6129 North Goshen Rd.
- **Clearcreek Country Club** is at 300 West Huntington Rd.
- **Etna Acres** is in Mount Etna, six miles south of Huntington.
- **Frazandanda** is on US 24, north of town.
- Quayle carries an eight handicap at **Congressional Country Club** in Bethesda, Maryland.
- Quayle also plays at **Burning Tree Country Club** and the **Tournament Players Club** at Avenel, Maryland.

STATUTE OF LIBERTY

They don't call this great country of ours the Land of Opportunity for nothing.

Uh, am I in the middle of a Shecky Greene routine?

Anyway, the "they" may be our friends south of the border because every day hundreds of them wade across the El Paso River or snip a hole in the hurricane fence to get to this great land of ours.

The most inviting spot on the US-Mexican border is the Yuma Desert outside Calexico, California. There is no river, no ditch, not even a fence. From I-8 take the Calexico exit south.

The spot on the US-Mexican border where the most illegal aliens have crossed into this great country is in the area around Brownsville, Texas, according to the Immigration and Naturalization Service. The aliens cross both upriver and downriver from town.

Brownsville is followed by El Paso (upriver or downriver), and San Diego (on the coast). For non-Mexicans, Brownsville is also the most popular, but San Diego is ahead of El Paso.

ATTACK OF THE KILLER BEES!

Bolt the windows and lock the doors! They're due any day now!

Killer bees!

Killer bees (real name: Africanized bees) are the Frankenstein monsters of the animal kingdom. They were created in 1957 when a Brazilian cross-breeding experiment went wrong. European bees were being bred with their more aggressive African cousins when several swarms escaped into the Brazilian countryside. By the early sixties Brazil's honeybees were almost all Africanized. Killer bees look identical to regular honeybees but they are angered more easily and attack more frequently. They've been expanding their territory at a rate of about three hundred miles a year.

And they are due in this country soon!

☆ **Getting There:** They are expected to cross the US-Mexican border somewhere in the eighty-mile stretch between Brownsville and La Joya, Texas. So set up a chair facing south and prepare for a long wait.

THE CASE OF THE OVERCONFIDENT BANDIT

This was really a case for Columbo: "Now let me get this straight . . . they stole what?"

A thief, or thieves, broke into the Family Planning Clinic at Grady Memorial Hospital in Atlanta in 1988 and made off with sixteen thousand condoms. For a daily user that's a forty-four year supply.

☆ **Getting There:** Grady Memorial Hospital is at 80 Butler St. in southeast Atlanta. Take I-75 south from downtown Atlanta. Get off at Exit 93, Martin Luther King Blvd. and the State Capitol, and bear right. (You'll be on Butler St.) Take a right at the third light on Butler St. (Butler St. dead-ends at that point.) The clinic is in Feebeck Hall, a red brick building.

MADE IN THE USA

—

If you are old enough to remember when comedians on the "Ed Sullivan Show" made jokes about things that were Made in Japan, boy are you old! About as old as I am, as a matter of fact. Now, of course, American-made products are the butts of jokes. But we still make some fine stuff here. Witness . . .

THE RUBBER CITY

Where do they make Trojans? If you said, Troy, Ohio, then you probably grew up in Dayton, where this is taken as fact.

Wrong.

And they don't make them in Akron, the Rubber City, either.

Trojan condoms, *the* name in rubbers, are manufactured in Trenton, New Jersey.

☆ **Getting There:** Carter-Wallace Company is at 310 Enterprise Ave. in Trenton, New Jersey. From Newark, take

Route 1 south. Where Route 1 splits (past Quaker Bridge Mall), bear left. At the Whitehead Rd. exit, make a right. Make another right at Second Ave. Second Ave. runs right into Enterprise. Sorry, no tours. Maybe if we start a letter-writing campaign that will change.

STRIPPERS

You've read about strip mines, the acne scars of the mountains. Maybe you've even seen pictures of mountains devastated by mining companies that dig what are effectively open mines. If you want to see how truly ugly strip mines are, you have to see them in person. Since you'll be in the Middlesboro, Kentucky, area anyway to see the cross-shaped home of Harrison Mayes (see What a Friend We Have in Jesus, page 240), you can extend your tour about a mile and see a strip mine, too.

Strip mines are a blight. And they are Made in the USA!

☆ **Getting There:** Take Cumberland Ave. (the main drag) through Middlesboro. Look left after you've gone through town and you'll see one of the best examples of twentieth-century strip mining.

ELVIS SPOTTED ON UFO!

That's a classic tabloid headline: it combines Elvis and UFOs, two tabloid favorites. When you talk tabloids, you're talking the *National Enquirer*, the top of the trash heap. The *Enquirer* publishes what inquiring—even nosy—minds want to know. And it's Made in the USA!

☆ **Getting There:** The *National Enquirer*'s newsroom is at 600 Southeast Coast Ave. in Lantana, Florida. Take I-95 and get off at Exit 46 (Lantana Rd.). Go east to Broadway and take a right. Go up six blocks and you'll see a bunch of Little League fields. If you take a left on any one of those side streets, you'll run right into the *National Enquirer* parking area. Sorry, no tours.

WHAT WE HAVE HERE IS A FAILURE TO SLOW DOWN

If you are old enough to remember the fifties, you are old enough to remember speed traps. Some small southern towns made their annual budgets on speeding fines extracted from northern billfolds that were on the way to Florida. (Of course, those northerners got revenge by charging southerners by the mile on northern toll roads.) The most notorious of all the speed traps according to AAA (the Automobile Association of America) was the one in Ludovici, Georgia. If they didn't get you for running the red light, they'd get you for exceeding the 35 mph speed limit.

The interstates changed all that.

☆ **Getting There:** From I-95 take Exit 13, SR 82 west to Ludovici. It's at the intersection of SR 82 and US 25-301. And observe posted speed limits.

BIGFEET,
TWO-HEADED BABIES,
AND LITTLE MEN FROM MARS

—

I once heard the respected television critic of a major national publication say of the *National Enquirer:* "You can't believe their two-headed baby stories, but when it comes to celebrity gossip, they are right on the money."

I was crushed. I always assumed the celebrity stuff was made up. But the stories of Bigfoot and friendly aliens? Come on. You can't make up stuff like that.

BIGFEET

It's impossible for me to tell you the exact spot to park and wait for a Bigfoot to appear. All I can do is give you some likely locations where these Sasquatch creatures have appeared before.

Bigfoot got his name from a road construction crew working in the Northern California mountains in 1958. They found footprints sixteen inches long and dubbed the creature who made them Bigfoot. The name stuck.

☆ **Getting There:** The crew was building SR 96 some twenty miles west of the town of Klamath River. From I-5 take SR 96 west toward the Klamath Mountains. Slow for Sasquatch.

On the East Coast there have been more sightings of Bigfoot in Pennsylvania than any other state. There were a large number of sightings in 1988 in the Chestnut Ridge Mountains between Derry and Ligonier.

☆ **Getting There:** From US 30 you can take SR 259 into the mountains. I accept no responsibility if you are killed or maimed by a Bigfoot.

BIGFOOT WITH SCALES

They call him the Lizard Man in the Lee County area of South Carolina. Because that's what he looks like. He's been spotted numerous times since 1985 in the Escape Ore Swamp of central South Carolina. In fact one man claimed to have grazed him with a gunshot. (He later confessed it was a hoax.)

Before you try to laugh this one off as another Abominable Snowman for rednecks, consider how seriously they view Lizard Man in South Carolina.

Columbia radio station WCOS has offered a $1-million reward for his capture.

And when state Republican party chairman Van Hipp passed out stickers at the 1988 GOP convention labeling Lizard Man a Democrat, he was warned off the stunt by some fellow delegates. One, Neal Thigpen, of Florence, told him, "Some local people take Lizard Man seriously. We shouldn't be putting a Democratic label on him because it could upset some folks."

☆ **Getting There:** The Lizard Man lives in the Escape Ore Swamp near Bishopville, South Carolina. From I-95 south toward Florence, South Carolina, take I-20 west toward Columbia. Get off at Exit 116; you'll be on US Highway

15. One mile ahead on the left, you'll see Brown Todd Rd.; go north . . . follow that road around three miles to the swamp.

LOCH HERRINGTON MONSTER

Not everybody in Kentucky's Jessamine and Mercer counties laughs when you ask about the Herrington Lake Monster. The monster, a fifteen-foot long creature with a pig snout and a curly tail and who-knows-what in between, isn't some ancient myth. University of Kentucky classics professor Lawrence Thompson first spotted "Herry" in 1972. He said she seemed to show herself early in the morning, before power boats took over the lake.

Herry has been explained as a giant catfish, a bobbing piece of driftwood, and a shadow from an unlighted fishing boat, but she has never been explained away. She has been spotted at Rocky Fork near Dix Dam and in the area between Chenault Bridge and Wells Landing. And even today fishermen return from the lake telling tales of Herry.

☆ **Getting There:** Head to Burgin, just east of Harrodsburg, Kentucky. At the junction of KY 33 and KY 152 take 33 north. A half mile from the crossroads, when 33 veers left, take Curdsville Rd. straight ahead for two and a half miles. Turn right at the Dix Dock sign. This is as close as you can get to Rocky Fork by land. It's off to the left, just out of sight.

OTHER MYSTERIOUS CREATURES

Champ, a black snakelike creature reported to be fifty feet long, lurks in New York's Lake Champlain. Joseph Zarzynski, head of the Lake Champlain Phenomena Investigation, has investigated 220 sightings. He thinks Champ is a plesiosaur, a dinosaur scientists say died out sixty million years ago.

☆ **Getting There:** Champ has been spotted as far north as Rouses Point, New York, and as far south as Whitehall, New York. Recent sightings have been clustered on the Vermont coast from Burlington south to Basin Harbor. To get to Basin Harbor take I-89 to US 7. Go south to SR 22A. Go west and follow signs to Basin Harbor.

Wallowa Lake Monster, which has seven humps and stretches fifty feet long, has been spotted in Wallowa Lake in eastern Oregon near Pendleton and La Grande.

☆ **Getting There:** From I-84 take SR 82 all the way to the lake. It's about seventy miles. The Wallowa Lake Monster Observation and Preservation Society Gala is held the third weekend in August at the south end of the lake. Call (503) 426-4074 for details.

The Jersey Devil, which has a horse's face, a kangaroo's body, a bat's wings, and a pig's hooves, haunts New Jersey's Pine Barrens. It's been seen by thousands of people including Admiral Farragut and Napoleon's brother.

☆ **Getting There:** Pine Barrens, also called the Pinelands, is 1.6 million acres of land in southern New Jersey. Start in Wharton State Park. From the Garden State Parkway take SR 542 west thirteen miles to Batsto.

KIDNAPPED BY SPACE ALIENS!

The first UFOs were spotted in the late forties, but it would be fifteen years before any of these visitors got friendly with the natives. The first claim of a UFO abduction was in 1961.

There are now about 150 people who say they have actually been inside one. The most famous of these close encounters happened to Barney and Betty Hill in September 1961 and was later turned into the 1975 TV movie *The UFO Incident*. Betty and Barney told police they were abducted in the White Mountains of New Hampshire by little men who looked a lot like Bob Hope.

The Hills were returning from a weekend vacation in Canada to their home in Portsmouth, New Hampshire, when they noticed they were being followed by a low-flying plane. Later they heard a strange beeping noise in their trunk and stopped to check it out. That's when Barney got a good look at the craft.

They drove on but were overtaken by drowsiness. The next thing they knew they were thirty-five miles down the road with no recollection of where they had been for the last two hours. It was not until they were hypnotized two years later that they remembered being taken up into the craft for examination and interrogation.

☆ **Getting There:** The Hills were driving on US 3 in the northern part of New Hampshire. They first spotted the UFO just before they got to Lancaster, which is near Berlin. They were taken on board the UFO near Indian Point in the White Mountains. They were returned to consciousness at the sign that reads "Concord 17 miles," near Ashland.

...AND A FREE PHYSICAL

The second most famous UFO abduction happened to a couple of Mississippi good old boys. Charles Hickson and Calvin Parker were fishing in the Pascaguola River one night in 1973 when an egg-shaped craft hovered over them and then took them on board. The two reported they were examined thoroughly before being floated back to the river bank. They became famous by telling the story on Tom Snyder's late night network talk show, "Tomorrow."

☆ **Getting There:** They were fishing at the mouth of the Pascaguola River within sight of the shipyard where they worked by day. From US 90, look south when you cross the Pascaguola River bridge.

SITE OF ONLY KNOWN GUN BATTLE BETWEEN ALIENS AND U.S. CITIZENS

Some say it never happened. Some say it happened, but not exactly the way you heard it. Danny McCord isn't sure.

"My aunt was a religious woman, and she swore to her dying day that it was aliens."

Whatever happened on that October night in 1955, it deeply affected the people in Kelly, a tiny community in south-central Kentucky.

Gaither McGehee, McGehee's wife and his sons, and a neighbor boy named Billy Ray Sutton were sitting in the McGehees' house when they saw a light in the field. It was large and bright and the commotion was loud and scary.

McGehee and his family would later claim that little green men leaped from the UFO that landed in the pasture and raced over to surround their house. What ensued was a wild and woolly shoot-out that belonged more to the Old West than to a twentieth-century Christian county.

The aliens retreated and flew away, leaving a house chunked with square bullet holes. And a public that was skeptical that anything but a drunken brawl had occurred.

But the sheriff told newspaper reporters, "These are not drinking people."

McCord concurs: "They were religious people." He says his uncle was so disturbed by the events of that night that he died a week later of a heart attack.

The house has been torn down. All that remains is the cistern. There is a bare spot in the field where the UFO landed. But it isn't bare from alien radiation. It's a garden patch, with tomato plants. McCord doesn't believe in UFOs, but he believed his aunt. "Like I say, I don't know what happened."

☆ **Getting There:** Kelly, Kentucky, is eight miles north of Hopkinsville. There is no town marker, just a highway sign that reads: "Congested Area, 45 mph." The only business in town is a bait shop that a fellow runs out of his house. To get to the shoot-out site turn east onto Kelly Chapel Rd.

Go across the railroad track and turn left at the Holiness church. After a half mile you'll see a block house, then two mobile homes. The spot is in the field just north of the second mobile home.

ON THE WHOLE

In October 1943 the U.S.S. *Eldridge,* a naval destroyer escort, headed out of the Philadelphia Navy Yard and vanished into the fog. Seconds later it reportedly appeared in the port facilities at Norfolk, Virginia, some 265 miles away. And in a few seconds it reappeared in Philadelphia. People who believe this story say the ship was part of a secret Navy experiment with force fields.

☆ **Getting There:** Philadelphia Navy Yard is south of town on the Delaware River. On I-95 at the Broad St. exit, look south and there it is.

FAMOUS MEAT SHOWER

On March 3, 1876, Mrs. Allan Crouch was in her yard in the shadow of Carrington Rock, in Bath County, Kentucky, making soap, when she was pummeled by meat falling from the heavens. It was thin-sliced, some of it still bloody, about a horse-wagonful of meat when it was loaded up and carted off.

It had been a clear, cloudless day. No tornado could have carried the meat to Carrington Rock. It was three decades before the Wright brothers' flight, so no airplane could have been involved.

The Meat Shower was investigated by Transylvania College professors and reporters from the *Louisville Commercial.*

It has never been explained.

☆ **Getting There:** Carrington Rock, Kentucky. From Interstate 64 take exit 123. Go south on KY 36 through Olympia to Olympia Springs. Carrington Rock is a large hill on the east side of the road three miles south of Olympia Springs, just across from a country store.

MOONWALKING, PART ONE

It was the early morning hours of July 20, 1969. Pajama-clad Americans were gathered around their TV sets watching as Neil Armstrong dropped from his ladder onto the moon's surface, uttering those famous words. ("That's one small step for a man," he said, not "That's one small step for man.") But not everyone watching believed that he was really on the moon. In fact there are still people who swear it was all staged in the Arizona desert. They say it was at Meteor Crater, just off I-40 east of Flagstaff. It does look

Where the Apollo moon landings were faked.

like the moon and it is where the Apollo lunar astronauts trained. Hmmm. I wonder. . . .

☆ **Getting There:** Meteor Crater is six miles off I-40 at Exit 233. It's $6 for adults, $5 if you tell them you are a member of AAA. (They don't ask to see your card; if you want to fib, that's between you and your God.) It isn't worth $5 unless you know about faking the Apollo landing there. It is open 6 A.M. to 6 P.M. local time.

A dead giveaway is all the Apollo 11 stuff in the souvenir shop.

MOONWALKING, PART TWO

He just wanted to shop for some rings in peace, for crying out loud. But what Michael Jackson got instead were peace officers. The disguised singer was so bizarre-looking with his wig, false mustache, false teeth and false eyelashes, that store employees at Zales Jewelry in Simi Valley, California, called the police. Jackson was questioned but no charges were filed after he revealed his identity.

☆ **Getting There:** Zales Jewelry is at 2914 Cochran St. in Simi Valley, California. From Highway 5 north, take Highway 118 west. Exit on Tapo St. and make a left at the first light. At the second light, make a right on Cochran. The store will be on the left side in the plaza.

OOPS!—ACCIDENTAL TOURIST SIGHTS

—

O h, these kids today. They have a tacky T-shirt that explains how they feel about life. It says: SH*T HAP-PENS (asterisk ours). They think their generation invented the Hilarious Goof (it was Spicoli in *Fast Times at Ridge-mont High* who invented it, they believe).

Wrong, children. Check out these sites of colossal blunders in history.

THIRTY SECONDS OVER SOUTH CAROLINA

On March 11, 1958, an Air Force B-47 bomber, en route from Hunter Air Force Base in Georgia to West Germany, accidentally dropped an atomic bomb on Walter Gregg's farm in the Mars Bluff community near Florence, South Carolina. The nonnuclear material exploded, leveling Gregg's farmhouse and leaving a crater seventy-five feet wide and thirty-five feet deep. No one was at home at the time. Five months later the Air Force settled with Gregg, paying him $54,000.

Folks around Florence now enjoy telling newcomers, "We were the town that got nuked."

☆ **Getting There:** The crater is now a swamp pond. Take Highway 76-301 east from Florence. Once you get past Francis Marion College, the next paved road to your right is Mars Bluff Rd. (you'll see the Mars Bluff lookout tower). The site where the crater was is about one mile down the road.

LOVE CANAL

It sounds like a bit of purple prose from a trash novel: Love Canal. "And as his hand slowly crept toward her . . ." Well, never mind.

But it was was the biggest environmental disaster of the seventies: an entire neighborhood contaminated by an old hazardous chemical dump.

A total of 717 families had to be relocated from the Love Canal neighborhood of Niagara Falls, New York, in 1978 because of seeping toxic waste from a former Hooker Chemical Company dump. The government has spent a quarter of a billion dollars cleaning up and resettling the area. In early 1989 it looked as if it might be for naught when more contamination was found in the Niagara Community Church parking lot, half a mile from the former Hooker Chemical Company dump site. But the hot spot was found to be no significant threat to residents. Three-quarters of the Love Canal neighborhood is now safe to live in, according to New York State's health commissioner, David Axelrod, who says the rest of the neighborhood may never be safe.

☆ **Getting There:** Today it's just a forty-acre mound of dirt encircled by a six-foot-high hurricane fence and a drainage ditch. Love Canal is six miles from downtown Niagara Falls. The dump is between Ninety-ninth and Ninety-seventh streets, which no longer exist in that area. A grand total of 43.6 million pounds of waste from the Hooker Chemical Company was dumped in Love Canal.

It's in the far eastern part of Niagara Falls. It's bordered by Ninety-third St., 100th St., Buffalo Ave., and Colbin Dr.

NUCLEAR POWER

Maybe you've seen the bumper sticker MORE PEOPLE HAVE DIED RIDING WITH TED KENNEDY THAN IN NUCLEAR ACCIDENTS. That was before Chernobyl, of course, but after Three Mile Island. In fact it was the meltdown at the Pennsylvania nuclear power plant and the ensuing hysteria that prompted pro–nuclear power types to make up the bumper stickers.

At about 4 A.M. on March 28, 1979, a relief valve at TMI-2 became stuck, releasing reactor cooling water as steam. Plant operators mistakenly shut off cooling water to the reactor. The core overheated and began a partial meltdown, producing a potentially explosive situation. Some 144,000 people were evacuated from the area at the same time that an equal number of journalists were rushing in to cover the story. But as the pronukies point out: no one died!

Three Mile Island: oops!

Times Beach, Missouri: Love Canal of the Midwest.

☆ **Getting There:** Three Mile Island Nuclear Power Plant is on a two-and-a-half-mile-long island in the Susquehanna River, twelve miles south of Harrisburg, Pennsylvania. Three Mile Island park and observation point is three miles south of Middletown, Pennsylvania, on SR 441.

LOVE CANAL OF THE MIDWEST

Times Beach, Missouri, is a town that has been wiped off the map. Literally. It's there in my 1984 atlas but it had disappeared by the 1988 edition. The deadly toxic waste dioxin was found in the soil of Times Beach and all the residents were relocated.

☆ **Getting There:** It's southwest of St. Louis. They've literally wiped it off the map. The exit on I-44 is unmarked. It's Exit 266, Lewis Rd. Go north until you come to a sign that reads: "Caution—hazardous waste site—dioxin contamination." No admittance without a permit. And they wouldn't give me one just for a little sight-seeing. Stay on the legal side of the gate. That's as close as you need to get to dioxin anyway.

JUST DON'T TRIP

You've heard of the San Andreas Fault, the plate intersection that will ultimately cause The Big One, the earthquake that topples California into the sea. How'd you like to walk along it? You can on the San Andreas Fault Trail in Palo Alto, California.

☆ **Getting There:** It's in the Los Trancos Open Space Preserve. From Palo Alto, take Page Mill Rd. south, past Highway 280, almost to Highway 35. (Highway 35 is Skyline Blvd., and if you get to it, you've gone too far.) There will be signs for Los Trancos Open Space Preserve parking. From Palo Alto, it's a long and winding road—it'll probably take forty-five minutes.

NO RICHTER TO GUIDE THEM

They pretty much had to start all over again in San Francisco after the earthquake of 1906. It devastated the town, razing four square miles of property, killing five hundred people, and ruining any chance of getting major league baseball for fifty years. They were just lucky they didn't have a Richter scale back then.

The epicenter of that deadly earthquake was at Olema, California, eleven miles north of Bolinas.

☆ **Getting There:** From US 101 take SR 1 north to Olema. Go to Bear Valley Visitors Center and look for the sign marking the epicenter.

VALLEY OF THE DRUMS

Next to Love Canal, this Kentucky site is probably the most famous toxic-waste dump in America. The Valley

comprises twenty-three acres with 17,000 visible drums
and an estimated 80,000 more underground. The drums
are filled with solid waste, liquid waste, every chemical
known to man: vinyl chloride, benzene, arsenic, PCBs,
you name it.

At the time of the Valley's discovery the Environmental Protection Agency termed it the nation's worst toxic-
dump site. But it has been cleaned up and is no longer on
the list of dumps eligible for clean-up money from the
federal government. For a look at an active dump, go three
miles farther down to Smith's Farm, where it is estimated
that as many as one million drums may have been dumped.

☆ **Getting There:** It's at 35600 National Turnpike, about fifteen miles south of Louisville, Kentucky. Take Interstate
65 south to Outer Loop west. Turn left on National Turnpike (KY 1020). Follow it into Bullitt County. Go just past
the L&N Golf Club and take the next right to the dump
site.

SUSAN SELLS WHAT BY THE SEASHORE?

New Jersey tourism took a beating in the summer of 1988.

The Jersey beaches were swamped, not with tourists,
but with medical waste, gross, disgusting medical waste:
syringes, blood vials, intravenous bags, and other medical
debris.

The floating refuse led to sporadic beach closings in
New Jersey and New York and reduced tourism by as
much as 50 percent. New Jersey officials claimed tourism
suffered a billion-dollar loss due to closed beaches.

Here's where to go and maybe find a blood-filled sy-
ringe or an AIDS-tainted blood bag:

NEW JERSEY BEACHES

• **Sandy Hook** was closed temporarily due to syringes.

• **Asbury Park** was closed temporarily due to high bac-
terial levels.

- **Cape May** was closed five days due to raw sewage.
- **Island Beach State Park** wasn't closed but an AIDS-tainted blood vial was found there in July 1988.

NEW YORK BEACHES

- **Rockaway Beach** in New York City was closed temporarily due to syringes and dead rats.
- **Jones Beach** was closed temporarily due to syringes and blood vials.
- **Long Beach** was closed temporarily due to syringes and blood vials.
- **Midland Beach** was closed temporarily due to raw sewage.
- **Atlantic Beach** on Long Island was closed three days due to raw sewage.
- **Coney Island Beach** in Brooklyn was closed three days due to raw sewage.
- **Manhattan Beach** was closed three days due to raw sewage.
- **Smith Point Beach** in Suffolk County, New York, was closed two days due to medical waste.
- **Fresh Kill Beach** on Staten Island was closed one day due to raw sewage.

OH SHIIIIIIIIIIIIIIIIII . . .

On March 19, 1980, Monica Meyers, the seventy-year-old mayor of Betterton, Maryland, was inspecting the city's municipal sewage treatment plant, testing the chlorine and sediment. She slipped on the catwalk, fell in, and drowned.

☆ **Getting There:** Take Route 292 into Betterton. Route 292 becomes Main St.; the sewage treatment plant is at the end of Third Ave.

HONEST, OFFICER, THERE USED TO BE A CAR DEALERSHIP HERE

One day it was a Porsche repair shop. The next day it was a hole.

That's what happened to the German Car Service in Winter Park, Florida. It was eaten by a sinkhole. Also devoured were a laundry, a printing company, and a three-bedroom house.

Mae Rose Owens, owner of the house, told the *St. Petersburg Times* that when she first reported the hungry sinkhole, police thought she had been drinking.

She had been outside feeding her dog, Muffin, when she observed a sixty-foot oak, followed by a trio of other trees, disappear. To combat nervousness she went inside to clean house. It helped the nerves, but not the house. Before the day was over her spotless house was also gone.

☆ **Getting There:** The Porsche repair shop was at 955 West Fairbanks Ave. The city has built up part of the property but the rest is a lake. In Winter Park, take the Fairbanks Ave. exit east from I-4.

FALLING STAR

In a certain light singer-dancer-actress-bombshell Ann-Margret has a put-together look to her. It's not Frankenstein-ugly, but it is definitely an artificially sculptured look. No, it isn't that she never learned how to put on makeup. It's that Ann-Margret was put back together.

In 1972 she fell twenty-two feet from a mechanical hand during rehearsal for her Lake Tahoe nightclub act and broke her face, crushing the left cheekbone so severely that it had to be rebuilt. She still looks good though.

☆ **Getting There:** Ann-Mar was playing the Sahara Lake Tahoe club at the time of her fall. It is now Del Webb's High Sierra on Highway 50 in South Shore—Lake Tahoe, Nevada.

CLEVELAND JOKES

Did you hear the one about the Cleveland mayor who caught his hair on fire at a ribbon-cutting ceremony?

How about the one about the Cleveland mayor whose wife skipped a White House dinner because it was her bowling night?

No, we're not going to give you more Cleveland jokes. We're going to give you Cleveland facts:

Cleveland mayor Ralph Perk did catch his hair ablaze while courting blue-collar workers. He was demonstrating his prowess with a blow torch. That's no joke.

And Perk did confess that his wife couldn't make the White House dinner because of her previous commitment. And that's no joke.

Cleveland is a fine town now but for years Cleveland was the butt of jokes by Johnny Carson. What made Cleveland a joke wasn't Perk's hair fire or his wife's bowling preference. It was the river catching fire.

In 1974 the Cuyahoga River, which runs through Cleveland, was so polluted you could stick a branch in it and the branch would stand upright. One summer evening the murky polluted mess finally caught fire. This event inspired singer-songwriter Randy Newman ("Short People") to pen the tune "Burn On, Big River, Burn On," which did not become a top-ten hit in Cleveland.

☆ **Getting There:** The Cuyahoga caught on fire six miles upstream at the railroad bridge. From I-77 take SR 21. Go over the river and look down. That's the spot.

SITE OF FIRST LSD EXPERIMENTS

The US Public Service Hospital in Bracktown, just north of Lexington, Kentucky, was where the psychedelic drug LSD was first tested on humans. Experiments were conducted on prisoners, all of them drug addicts, at the Hospital's Addiction Research Center from 1953 to 1962 and were funded by the CIA.

Some three hundred prisoners were given LSD, many of them unaware of what they were receiving. Because there was no budget to pay the human guinea pigs, the reward was a choice: time off their sentences or the drug of their choice. Since they were addicts, most chose the drug. One prisoner told a Senate subcommittee that he received morphine for his participation. Pennsylvania Senator Richard Schweiker replied, "I understand now why the percentage cure at Lexington may not have been too high."

☆ **Getting There:** From Lexington take US 421, Leestown Pike, north. The old hospital is on the right, just past Masterson Station Park. It is now the Federal Correction Institute. You can see all you need to see from the road.

DEAD WRONG

It had been a hard-fought battle at Spotsylvania Courthouse, but finally it looked as if the tide was turning in favor of the Union. They were even getting a little cocky behind federal lines. General John Sedgewick peered out at enemy lines and bragged to his aide, "What, what men! This will never do, dodging for single bullets. I tell you they could not hit an elephant at this d—"

Unfortunately for General Sedgewick, they weren't shooting at elephants. He died instantly from a bullet wound to the head.

☆ **Getting There:** Spotsylvania Courthouse is seven miles south of Fredericksburg on SR 738.

THE LAND OF LOST LUGGAGE

If you still have occasional nagging thoughts about that Nehru jacket you lost years ago when the airline put you on one flight and your luggage on another, there's still hope. Most lost luggage in this country is sold to a couple of unclaimed freight stores in Scottsboro, Alabama: T&W Unclaimed Baggage Outlet and Unclaimed Baggage Center, across the street.

☆ **Getting There:** T&W is at 506 West Willow St. Take Highway 79 to downtown Scottsboro. Take a left at the third light. Approximately four blocks later, take a right at the stop sign. Approximately five blocks later, turn right at the light. At this point you will be able to see the store—a long, low building. (*Note:* Stay on Highway 79 when it turns into Highway 279 before you get to Scottsboro; do *not* take the bypass.) The store is open on Wednesdays and Saturdays only. Unclaimed Baggage Center is across the street. It is open every day except Sunday.

VOLCANO!

It was like an Irwin Allen movie, only you didn't have to put up with Charlton Heston. It was the eruption of the Mount St. Helens volcano in Washington state in May 1980. Thirty-six died in the disaster. Another twenty-one were never found. The prospects of it erupting while you are visiting are slim, but there is a museum and a souvenir shop.

☆ **Getting There:** The Mount St. Helens Museum is at 9449 Spirit Lake Highway. From Highway 5 take Highway 504. It's nineteen miles. There's also a visitors center and you can climb to the top. Call (206) 274-4038 for details.

WHY DO YOU THINK THEY CALL THEM SKYSCRAPERS?

If you've ever traced the path of a low-flying plane across the sky and wondered why they never crash into skyscrapers, the answer is "Occasionally they do." In fact on July 28, 1945, a veteran army pilot lost his bearings in the fog and crashed his plane into the side of New York City's Empire State Building, at that time the tallest building in the world. Fortunately it was a Saturday so there were few people in the building or on the sidewalk below. Still eleven people in the building and on the ground and three in the plane died.

☆ **Getting There:** The Empire State Building is at 350 Fifth Ave. The plane crashed into the seventy-eighth floor. That's twenty-four floors from the top.

SPARE-ROOM MUSEUMS

———

Something there is about someone who is so fanatical about his hobby that he puts together a display in his spare room. I think these are the best kinds of museums because the curator is hovering right there, ready, willing, even anxious to answer all your questions.

———

EXOTIC WORLD

She was one of the biggest stars of the business. She was so big, in fact, that they nicknamed her "The Bazoom Girl." But those days are behind her, sort of, and today stripper Jenny Lee, fifty-seven, is retired. But she still has an intense interest in the world of exotic dancing. She keeps her hands in the field by maintaining a stripper museum in her home.

Curator Lee, who was in the film *Three Nuts in Search of a Bolt* in 1963 with Mamie Van Doren, has a sizable collection of historic G-strings, inflatable party dolls, posters, and boob novelty items.

She even has Jayne Mansfield's old heart-shaped couch.

Her Hall of Dames photo gallery includes portraits of such greats of the field as Morganna, Honey Bruce, and Chesty Morgan.

☆ **Getting There:** Tours are by appointment only. Call (619) 948-1153 or (619) 243-5261. Admission is $10 and includes a souvenir pack with a photo of Jenny signed "Bust wishes." The address is 29053 Wild Rd., Helendale, California, which is in the desert northeast of Los Angeles.

From Highway 15 in Victorville, take a left onto D St., which runs into Old National Trails Highway. Take Old National Trails Highway north fifteen miles to the Helendale Market. Turn left on Vista St. and go two miles to a pair of artificial waterfalls. That is Helendale Rd. Go one mile to Wild Rd., then another mile to the iron gates. Exotic World is near the Roy Rogers Museum, which might be worth a side trip just to see stuffed Trigger.

Jenny asks that if you write to the museum requesting information, "Please send a SASE (self-addressed stamped envelope)." She says she gets a lot of mail.

NOT AFFILIATED WITH THE CHAMBER OF COMMERCE

The Tragedy in U.S. History Museum in St. Augustine, Florida, is what this book is all about. I remember reading an article years ago describing the problems museum owner L. H. "Buddy" Hough was having with the St. Augustine Chamber of Commerce. They wouldn't let him put his brochure in their office. It didn't fit in with their image of St. Augustine.

And I remember wondering what other great tourist sights might be out there, struggling to make ends meet because the local Chamber didn't approve. And the end result is this book.

What Buddy Hough has assembled is a collection of tacky relics: Jayne Mansfield's death car, Lee Harvey Oswald's boarding house furniture, the car Oswald rode to work the morning of the assassination. Good stuff in other words.

There's the ambulance that carried Oswald to the hospital after he was shot, along with an autographed photo of ambulance driver Red Yager and Oswald's pocket comb. (The authenticity of all the Oswald artifacts is vouched for by Oswald's landlady, Mary Bledose, in a conspicuous letter. Hough got the stuff in a straight swap by fixing her porch roof.)

☆ **Getting There:** It is at 7 Williams St. in St. Augustine, Florida. From I-95 take state Route 16 to east San Marco Ave. (seven miles). Go south one block to Williams and left on Williams.

ORAL PLEASE

You can thrill to the excitement of two hundred years of thermometers at the Thermometer Museum in Sacramento.

Or you can wonder why anyone would have two hundred years of thermometers.

☆ **Getting There:** The Thermometer Museum is at 4555 Auburn Blvd., Suite 11, in Sacramento, California. Call (916) 487-6964 for an appointment (required). From Placerville, take I-50 west to Sacramento. Exit on Watt Ave. Go north on Watt for twenty to twenty-five minutes (go toward north Sacramento); take a right on Auburn Blvd. Stay on Auburn Blvd. for five to six minutes until you see Oak Furniture Store on the left. Turn in there and go around to the back; the museum is next to RPM Auto.

YES, WE HAVE A BANANA MUSEUM

Everything bananas is at the Banana Museum. Everything. From banana earrings, banana pipes, and banana clocks to a six-foot stuffed banana and a Michael Jackson sequined banana. More than 14,000 banana items.

☆ **Getting There:** It's at 2524 North Elmolina in Altadena, California. It's two and a half miles north of the 210 Freeway in Altadena (a small community north of Pasadena).

GOOD VIBRATIONS

You can look at (but you better not touch) such marvels of early vibrator technology as the Marvolotor, the Handy Hannah, and the Vim at San Francisco's Vibrator Museum.

They even have a hand-crank model that looks like an egg beater. It illustrates the lengths (and depths) people went to before electricity became commonplace.

☆ **Getting There:** The Vibrator Museum is at Good Vibrations, 1210 Valencia, in the Mission district of San Francisco. Take 101 north to the Mission St. off ramp. Go straight through one light and make a left at the second light (onto Valencia). Go to Twenty-second St. and make a right; museum will be eight to ten blocks down at 1210 Valencia. Call (415) 550-7399 for information. The museum is actually just a couple of shelves on a wall.

WEIRD LIBRARY COLLECTIONS

Before Ronald Reagan became famous for his prematurely orange hair there was Rudy Vallee and his magenta mop.

The formula for the late Rudy Vallee's hair dye along with X-rays of his impacted wisdom tooth and other exciting memorabilia can be found in the Thousand Oaks Library's archive on the history of radio and early television.

☆ **Getting There:** From Los Angeles, take the Ventura Freeway (101) west through the San Fernando Valley. Pretty soon you will see signs for Agoura Hills, then Westlake Hills, and then Thousand Oaks. Take Filmore exit (Exit 23); you have to go right. Take the Janss exit; go right at the bottom of the ramp. After about a half a block, you'll see a long driveway that leads to a large white modern building with a slanted roof; that building is the library.

MASS MEDIA MURDER SITES

——

R emember the first time you heard a perfectly coiffed TV reporter talking about a serial killer? Did you think he was referring to Post Toasties or Corn Flakes?

Now the mass media have made the term "serial killer" a household word. In fact it is no longer enough to call a suspect a serial killer. Now the unknown killer has to have a nickname, something catchy for the masses: The Hillside Strangler, The Night Stalker, The Green River Killer.

This chapter will put you on the trail of some of our most media-wise serial killers and other well-known murderers.

RICHARD SPECK

Richard Speck, who strangled and stabbed eight student nurses in Chicago on July 14, 1966, is generally considered the first of the modern mass murderers. Speck, then twenty-four, was convicted of murder and sentenced to

death. The death sentence was removed when the Supreme Court struck down all death sentences.

☆ **Getting There:** The murders occurred at 2319 East 100th
St. on the South Side of Chicago.

CHARLES WHITMAN

"There was a rumor, he had a tumor . . ." was a lyric from
a Kinky Friedman song in the late sixties. The song was
about Charles Whitman, the psycho who climbed the University of Texas tower in 1966, two weeks after Speck's
spree, and shot twenty-nine people, killing fourteen of
them, including Charles Boyer, a scientist working on the
black hole theory. Earlier Whitman had killed his wife and
his mother. Police shot him to death in the tower.

☆ **Getting There:** From I-35 take Martin Luther King, Jr.,
Blvd. west to Lamar Blvd. Go north to the campus. You'll
see the tower. Don't flinch when you do.

SON OF SAM

Initially the newspapers called him the .44-Caliber Killer,
named for his gun. But soon the killer let them know what
they should call him. In a block-print letter to police that
demonstrated poor spelling skills, he wrote: "I am deeply
hurt by your calling me a wemon hater. I am not. But I am
a monster. I am 'Son of Sam.' "

Before David Berkowitz, the twenty-four-year-old
postal worker, was caught on August 10, 1977, he had shot
thirteen people, killing seven of them.

Donna Lauria was his first victim. She was killed on
July 29, 1976, as she exited a double-parked Oldsmobile
in front of 2860 Buhre Ave. in Pelham Bay in the northeast
Bronx. Her friend Jody Valente was wounded in the leg.

Carl Denaro was shot in the head near the corner of

159th St. and Thirty-third Ave. in Flushing, Queens. He survived.

Joanne Lomino and Donna DeMasi were shot in the yard in front of the Lomino home on 262nd St. in Queens, between Hillside and Eighty-first Ave. Although seriously wounded, both survived.

Christine Freund was killed in her boyfriend's car in Station Plaza, near the Long Island Railroad tracks and Continental Ave. in Queens.

Virginia Voskerichian was killed in front of 4 Dartmouth St. in Forest Hills, New York.

Valentina Suriani and her boyfriend, Alexander Esau, were murdered as they necked in a car parked on the shoulder of the Hutchinson River Parkway opposite 1878 Hutchinson River Parkway.

Judy Placido was shot in a parked car on 211th St. near the intersection with Forty-fifth Rd. in Queens. Her companion was injured in the wrist. Placido survived.

Stacy Moskowitz and Robert Violante were shot in a parked car on the Shore Parkway service road in Bensonhurst, just across from Bay 17th. Moskowitz died.

Berkowitz's car had been ticketed for illegal parking only minutes before his last murder, which is how he was finally caught. He had parked his Ford Galaxie in front of 290 Bay 17th.

He is currently serving his term at Attica Correctional Facility in upstate New York.

JOHN WAYNE GACY

The man actually convicted of more murders than anyone else is John Wayne Gacy, convicted in 1979 of killing thirty-three young men and boys between 1972 and 1978. The bodies of twenty-seven were discovered in the crawl space underneath Gacy's home.

☆ **Getting There:** Gacy's home was at 1321 Apert Lane in Norwood Park, Illinois, a Chicago suburb. Take exit 81-A from I-90.

FYI: Juan Corona is second only to Gacy in the number of murders he was convicted of: twenty-five. He is serving twenty-five consecutive life sentences for the murders of twenty-five itinerant farm workers in California in 1971. Corona, a farm supervisor at the time, was convicted of killing the migrant farm workers he had hired and burying them near the Feather River at Yuba City, California.

He is currently incarcerated in Soledad Prison. (See Celebrity Hard Time, page 185, for directions.)

Yuba City is about an hour north of Sacramento on SR 99. The scene of the crime is now private property and for some reason they don't want tourists.

JAMES HUBERTY

On July 18, 1984, Huberty, an unemployed security guard, shot and killed twenty people in the McDonald's restaurant in San Ysidro, California. He was shot to death by police.

☆ **Getting There:** McDonald's razed the restaurant and playground. Now on the site is a continuing education college. The Yum Yum Donut Shop, which was next door, is still there. It's at 428 San Ysidro Blvd. From San Diego, take I-5 south; exit at Dairymart. Cross the bridge, make a right, and the doughnut shop is right there.

THE HILLSIDE STRANGLER

When the bodies of ten young women were found raped and strangled to death in the hillsides of northeast Los Angeles in the last months of 1977, the media had a new mass murderer: The Hillside Strangler. Then in the spring of 1978, as mysteriously as he had begun, the Strangler ended his reign of terror. No new bodies were found. The Strangler, or one half of the Strangler team, Kenneth Bianchi, had moved to Bellingham, Washington, where he was apprehended after strangling two women.

He snitched on his first cousin, Angelo Buono, in a plea-bargain on the Bellingham deaths. Buono was eventually convicted of nine of the ten Hillside Strangler deaths. He is serving a life sentence without possibility of parole. After Bianchi reneged on his deal to testify against Buono, the judge reneged on the deal to let him serve his time in California and shipped him back to Washington State Prison in Walla Walla.

☆ **Getting There:** According to Bianchi, most of the Strangler murders were committed at Buono's home and upholstery shop at 703 East Colorado St. in Los Angeles. From I-5 (Golden State Freeway) take the Colorado St. exit east. Buono's home has since been razed, but the upholstery shop, which was in the rear, remains. It is on the north (left) side of the street.

MURDERER'S ROW

The so-called Green River Killer, blamed for at least forty murders in the Tacoma, Washington, area since 1980 and still at large, has frequently preyed on prostitutes and runaways that he found on a stretch of Highway 99 near the Seattle-Tacoma airport. Many of the victims' bodies were found in the Green River.

☆ **Getting There:** If you want to see the spot where he dumped a couple of bodies, go south on I-5 from the airport. When you get to the bridge (and the sign that says "Green River"), underneath that point is what you're looking for.

I don't have the space, or the stomach, to detail all forty sites.

THE BLACK DAHLIA

Elizabeth Short was a small-town dreamer who came to Hollywood in the forties, seeking fame and fortune. She

hung around the fringes of the movie business but didn't
find fame until her gruesome death in 1947. On the morning of January 15, 1947, her mutilated body was found in a
vacant lot in west Los Angeles. It was ten days before she
was identified, and during that time she was referred to as
the Black Dahlia. Her murder remains unsolved.

☆ **Getting There:** From I-10 (the Santa Monica Freeway)
take the Crenshaw exit south to Thirty-ninth St. Go east
two blocks to Norton, then north to the middle of the
block. Her body was found in the vacant lot on the west
side of the street about halfway between Thirty-ninth and
Coliseum streets.

THE PREPPIE MURDER

In the early morning hours of August 26, 1986, Robert
Chambers and Jennifer Levin left Dorrian's Red Hand, an
Upper East Side bar in Manhattan. Hours later her lifeless

The Preppie Murder bar: Dorrian's Red Hand.

body was found in Central Park. The media quickly dubbed it the Preppie Murder case because of Levin's upper-middle-class upbringing.

Chambers would later claim he accidentally strangled Levin during a round of "rough sex." He pleaded guilty to manslaughter and is serving five to fifteen years at the Great Meadow Correctional Facility in Comstock, New York.

☆ **Getting There:** Dorrian's Red Hand is at 300 East 84th St.

The murder site is in Central Park behind the Metropolitan Museum of Art.

ON THE ROAD WITH CHARLES STARKWEATHER

Before Charlie Whitman and Charlie Manson, there was Charlie Starkweather, a James Dean—like character who went on a ten-day rampage of death and destruction in the winter of 1958.

Although his exploits have been romanticized by the media, including the 1973 film *Badlands,* the fact remains that Starkweather killed almost a dozen people before he and his fourteen-year-old girlfriend, Caril Ann Fugate, were captured.

The ten days of terror began on January 21, 1958, when Charlie shot and killed girlfriend Caril Ann's mother, stepfather, and half-sister at 924 Belmont Avenue in Lincoln, Nebraska.

Here's the route he and Caril Ann took during their rampage.

On Monday, January 27, they left the Belmont Avenue house, went to a gas station, then to a garage on Twenty-sixth and Ragsdale, then to Dale's Champion Service to get the car worked on. They left there and headed out Highway 77 past the Nebraska State Penitentiary to Bennett, Nebraska, where they killed farmer August Meyer and teenagers Robert Jensen and Carol King. They headed west on Highway 6 to Hastings, then, inexplicably, they turned around and headed back to SR 6 to Lincoln.

They killed industrialist C. Lauer Ward, his wife, Clara Ward, and their maid, Lillian Fencl, at the Ward home on South 24th Street in the Country Club estates section of Lincoln.

By now Charlie and Caril Ann were notorious fugitives and the objects of a statewide hunt.

They knew they had to get out of Lincoln, but before they did, they drove past the house on Belmont again and headed west on Highway 34. In Grand Island they turned on Highway 2 toward the Sand Hills. They went through Broken Bow, Ellsworth, and Crawford, where they turned west onto Highway 20.

The drove to Douglas, Wyoming, where they took Highway 87 toward Caspar. About eleven miles west of Douglas they found traveling shoe salesman Merle Collison asleep in his car. Charlie killed him and was trying to steal his car when a geologist from Caspar, thinking he was having car trouble, stopped to help. Charlie threatened the man and a struggle ensued. A policeman who happened by stopped to see what was going on. Caril Ann ran to the police car and told the deputy it was Charlie Starkweather. The end of the rampage was near.

Charlie ran back to his car and headed back to Douglas, with two deputies in hot pursuit. They raced through downtown Douglas at 100 mph until they were caught in a traffic jam. At the traffic light in the center of town the deputy shot at Charlie's tires. Pedestrians hit the ground. But Charlie managed to elude his pursuers. On the open highway outside town a deputy shot out Charlie's rear window. Charlie continued on about half a mile, then stopped in the dead center of the road and surrendered.

He and Caril Ann were in Converse County jail overnight.

She was eventually sentenced to life imprisonment at the Nebraska Center for Women at York. She was released in 1976. Charlie was executed at the Nebraska State Penitentiary in Lincoln on June 25, 1959.

☆ **Getting There:** Take Highway 77 south to Highway 2 to Bennett, then backtrack to Highway 6 to Hastings. Return to Lincoln on Highway 6. Take Highway 34 to Grand Island and Highway 2 all the way to Crawford in the northwest corner of the state. Then head west on Highway 20 to Douglas, Wyoming, where you head toward Caspar. Eleven miles west of Douglas, turn around and head back. Just east of Douglas on old Highway 20 was where Charlie was captured.

The Nebraska State Penitentiary is on Highway 77 in Lincoln. Follow Ninth St. south all the way down past "O" St., past Van Dorn, past the McDonald's (and a park). The State Pen is right on the corner of Highway 77 and Highway 2; it's a big brick building with a big fence—you can't miss it.

Nebraska Center for Women is in York. From the interstate, get off at the York exit and go north. When you get to Fourth St., go west until you see the center.

THE RED LIGHT BANDIT

Caryl Chesman doesn't really belong in a section with murderers. He was not a murderer but a rapist and robber. His career as the Red Light Bandit—so called because he used a spotlight that made his car look like a police car—lasted only three weeks. But in that time he committed at least eighteen crimes, including robbery, kidnapping, grand theft auto, and rape. He was eventually convicted of seventeen of those counts and sentenced to the gas chamber. He was executed at San Quentin in 1960 for the crime of "kidnapping with great bodily harm."

☆ **Getting There:** He was caught at the corner of Sixth and Shatto in Los Angeles. Take the Vermont St. exit south from the Hollywood Freeway. Turn left and go one block to Shatto.

BEST-SELLING MURDER SITES

—

Publishers *Weekly* credits Truman Capote with creating the true-crime genre with *In Cold Blood,* which was published in 1965. Since then scarcely a drop of blood has fallen on an American sidewalk that an agent didn't run up asking if subsidiary rights had been sold yet.

Here, in the spirit of Cliff Notes and *True Detective* magazine, is a guide to the scenes of the crimes of some of these best-selling murders.

IN COLD BLOOD BY TRUMAN CAPOTE

In 1959 two small-time hoodlums, Perry Smith and Richard Hickock, invaded a home in Holcomb, Kansas, and killed all four members of the Clutter family.

☆ **Getting There:** From I-70 take US 83 south toward Garden City. Take US 50 west to Holcomb. The Clutters lived on the River Valley Farm on River Rd. The farm is back off the road, surrounded by a lifetime supply of "Private

Property—No Trespassing" signs. Don't even consider driving down the road.

THE BOSTON STRANGLER BY GEROLD FRANK

In the eighteen months between June 1962 and January 1964 Boston was stalked by a maniac who strangled single women to death. His modus operandi had police baffled. All the women were strangled with their own clothing. There were no signs of forcible entry. And nothing was stolen. Before Albert DeSalvo was captured he had killed thirteen women.

☆ **Getting There:** On the trail of the Boston Strangler (addresses are in Boston unless otherwise noted):

- Ann Slessers was murdered at 77 Gainsborough St.
- Mary Mullen was strangled at 1435 Commonwealth Ave.
- Nina Nichols died at 1940 Commonwealth Ave.
- Helen Blake was killed at 73 Newhall St. in Lynn.
- Ida Irga died at 7 Grove St.
- Jane Sullivan was murdered at 435 Columbia Rd.
- Sophie Clark was strangled at 315 Huntingdon Ave.
- Patricia Bissette died at 515 Park Dr.
- Mary Brown was murdered at 319 Park Ave. in Lawrence.
- Beverly Samans was killed at 4 University Rd. in Cambridge.
- Evelyn Corbin was strangled at 224 Lafayette St. in Corbin.
- Joann Graff died at 54 Essex St. in Lawrence.
- Mary Sullivan was murdered at 44A Charles St.
- DeSalvo lived at 11 Florence St. Park in Malden, Mass.

There are so many addresses here it would be best if you buy your own map of Boston.

BLOOD AND MONEY BY THOMAS THOMPSON

Houston plastic surgeon Dr. John Hill was accused of injecting a fatal dose of bacteria into his wife's bloodstream in 1969. After his prosecution ended in a mistrial, Dr. Hill turned up dead, shot to death in his own home. And all fingers pointed to his former father-in-law, millionaire oilman Ash Robinson.

☆ **Getting There:** John and Joan Hill lived at 1561 Kirby Dr. in Houston. Ash lived down the street at 1029 Kirby. From the Katy Freeway (I-10) take Durham Dr. south to Kirby. Go right on Kirby.

FATAL VISION BY JOE McGINNISS

Writer McGinniss was almost a part of the defense team for army captain and former Green Beret Dr. Jeffrey MacDonald, who was charged with savagely killing his wife and two daughters in a knife attack at their home on an army base in 1970. McGinniss even shared royalties with MacDonald. So when McGinniss's book concluded that MacDonald was guilty, there was a little bad blood. And a big lawsuit.

☆ **Getting There:** The home is at 544 Castle Dr. on the Fort Bragg army base. It's near Fayetteville, North Carolina. MacDonald was convicted. (See Celebrity Hard Time, page 185 for his current whereabouts.)

HELTER SKELTER BY VINCENT BUGLIOSI

The notorious Manson murders were actually two nights of mayhem that occurred August 9 and 10, 1969. Killed in the first attack were actress Sharon Tate, twenty-six, coffee

heiress Abigail Folger, twenty-five, her boyfriend, Woji-
ciech Frykowski, thirty-two, hairdresser Jay Sebring,
thirty-five, Steven Parent, eighteen, an unfortunate by-
stander who was a friend of the mansion's caretaker, and
Tate's unborn son. They were at a party at the Hollywood
Hills mansion that Tate and her husband, director Roman
Polanski, were renting, when the Manson followers burst
in and slaughtered them.

The next night grocery store executive Leno La-
Bianca, forty-four, and his wife Rosemary, thirty-eight,
were butchered at their home on Waverly Drive. The Manson folks wrote "Death to Pigs" on the walls and, demonstrating poor spelling skills, "Healter Skelter" on the
refrigerator. Then they showered and had a bite to eat
before escaping.

Manson follower Susan Atkins later testified that she,
Leslie Van Houten, Patricia Krenwinkel, Tex Watson, and
Linda Kasabian had committed the killings at the orders of
Charlie. And that Manson himself had tied up the La-
Biancas before directing Watson, Krenwinkel, and Van
Houten to kill them.

☆ **Getting There:** The Tate killings were at 10050 Cielo Dr.
The LaBianca home was at 3301 Waverly Dr. It was recently on the market for $599,000.

To the Tate murder scene: From Sunset Blvd. in Beverly Hills take Benedict Canyon Rd. north to Cielo. Go left
to a private street near the corner of Davies Rd. It is at the
end of the private drive but don't go down there.

To the LaBianca murder scene: From I-5 (San Diego
Freeway) take Glendale Blvd. south. (If you are coming
from downtown you have to go north. You can make a U-
turn a few blocks up.) Turn right on Rowena, go three
blocks to Waverly. Turn right. Just past the convent, on the
left, is 3311, the LaBianca home. It was 3301 in 1969 but
the house number has been changed.

BITTER BLOOD BY JERRY BLEDSOE

In the summer of 1984 Delores Lynch and her daughter Janie were found shot to death at her quiet country home east of Louisville, Kentucky. Months later Robert, Florence, and Hattie Newsom were found murdered in their Winston-Salem, North Carolina, home. The connection was Susie Lynch, daughter of Robert and Florence Newsom, granddaughter of Hattie Newsom, and former daughter-in-law of Delores Lynch. The murders were a result of a bitter divorce and custody battle. Susie had fallen in with her gun-nut cousin Fritz Klenner, who led her down the road to murder and suicide. Of course, no one made her follow.

☆ **Getting There:** To the Kentucky murder site: from I-71 north east of Louisville take I-265 (Exit 9) north until it dead-ends into US 42. Go right three miles to Covered Bridge Rd. (just past the Five Star Market). Go right on Covered Bridge four miles. The address is 10420 State Rte. 329. It's on the right.

To the Winston-Salem murder site: from I-40 take the Silas Creek Parkway north to Reynolda Rd. Go left for two miles. Three blocks past the Pine Ridge Shopping Center turn left onto Valley Rd. It's at 3239 Valley Rd.

The end for Fritz, Susie, and her two boys came after a bizarre death chase through Greensboro. Fritz blew up the Chevy Blazer they were in, killing all four. The final chase began at Susie's apartment, 28-L Hunt Club Rd. in the Friendly Hills Apartments. They traveled east on Friendly Ave., turning north on New Garden Rd., north again on US 220, and east on SR 150. The explosion occurred on Highway 150 between Bronco Lane and Strader Rd.

NUTCRACKER BY SHANA ALEXANDER

Thomas Thompson was working on *Nutcracker* when poor health forced him to give it up and turn over his notes to former *Life* magazine co-worker Alexander. It's the story of spoiled rich girl Frances Schreuder, who in 1978 ordered her son to kill her father. Money was the root of the problem. Frances wanted her inheritance now.

☆ **Getting There:** The murder was in a warehouse at 337 Pierpoint Ave. in Salt Lake City.

THE STRANGER BESIDE ME BY ANN RULE

We'll never know how many people psychopath Ted Bundy killed. In the hours before his execution in 1989 he began rattling off more and more names in hopes of postponing the inevitable. In the end the government decided it would rather fry him than listen to him dredging up murder memories. The best estimate is that he killed at least forty people, most of them women, in the Northwest and Florida.

Rule, who knew him very well in the early seventies, chronicles his murder spree.

☆ **Getting There:** Bundy lived for five years at 4143 Twelfth St. NE in Seattle, Washington. He also lived at 565 First Ave., No. 2 in Salt Lake City.

At the Florida State Penitentiary, near Starke, he was electrocuted in Old Sparky, a three-legged oak chair. Bundy was the 216th person to die in the chair since its installation in 1923. It was constructed by prison inmates.

ECHOES IN THE DARKNESS BY JOSEPH WAMBAUGH

This is perhaps the most bizarre true crime story ever told: a high school principal and an English teacher, apparently at odds, conspire to murder another teacher for insurance money. I don't have the space to get into all the twists and turns in the story of murderers William Bradfield and Jay Smith.

☆ **Getting There:** The body of teacher Susan Reinert was found in the trunk of her Plymouth Horizon, which was parked in the front lot of the American Host Inn near Harrisburg. Her two children were never found. The Americana Host Inn is now the Holiday Inn East. It is at 4751 Lindle Rd. in Harrisburg, Pennsylvania. Take the Pennsylvania Turnpike to the Harrisburg exit. Take Highway 283 north to the Swatara exit. Take a right at the stop sign; the hotel will be on the right-hand side.

William Bradford, Susan Reinert, and Jay Smith all worked at Upper Merion Senior High School. It's at 435 Crossfield Rd. in King of Prussia, Pennsylvania. Take the Pennsylvania Turnpike to the Valley Forge exit; go straight ahead to 202 north. Head up the hill; you'll go through one light and see a Hilton on the right. Turn left at the next light at Town Center Road. Make a left at the T intersection onto Prince Frederic Rd. Make a left on Crossfield.

SMALL SACRIFICES BY ANN RULE

Diane Downs said she loved her children. But the man she wanted didn't want to be a daddy. And she could always have more children. So in 1983 she decided to solve her problem with a gun.

☆ **Getting There:** Downs shot her children at the end of Old Mohawk Rd. in Marcola, Oregon. One died; the other two lived despite serious injuries.

BLIND FAITH BY JOE MCGINNISS

This is the story of a man who killed his wife for money: insurance money. Maria Marshall was murdered in 1984 by husband Rob in the Oyster Creek picnic area off the Garden State Parkway, some ten miles south of Toms River, New Jersey.

☆ **Getting There:** It's the first rest area south of Exit 74.

CELEBRITY HARD TIME

—

Once upon a time going to prison was a disgrace. Now it is a career move.

In the recent past our prisons have been flooded with celebrity prisoners, there to pay their small debt to society so they can return to collect on the larger debts society owes them: the Jake Butchers and Ivan Boeskys from the world of finance, the Ray Blantons and John Jenrettes from the world of politics, the Denny McClains and Hollywood Hendersons from the world of sports. Name a world, somewhere out there it's represented by a celebrity prisoner.

This new class of prisoner has been met with a new class of prison: the minimum-security prison farm. Don't put too much stock in the "farm" part.

Country club might be a better term.

But before you start criticizing, be aware that even celebrity prisoners have to pay some price, however small. At Allenwood in Pennsylvania each prisoner must share a small cubicle with another prisoner. Grounds detail, the most popular prison job, pays just eleven cents an hour. At neighboring Lewisburg Federal Penitentiary the prisoners maintain 954 acres outside the walls working 7:45 A.M. until 3:45 P.M.

CELEBRITY PRISONERS

Here's where some of your favorite celebrity prisoners are or were serving their hard time:

Wall Street inside trader **Ivan Boesky**—the man who actually said "Greed is healthy"—is still serving at this writing at the Lompoc Camp, Lompoc, California, north of Los Angeles.

Sirhan Sirhan, convicted murderer of Robert Kennedy, is serving his life sentence in Soledad Prison, Soledad, California.

Everyone's favorite mass murderer, **Charles Manson,** is in Corcoran Prison, a new maximum-security prison in Kings County, California. He becomes eligible for parole again in 1992. He has been denied parole seven times already.

Mark David Chapman, John Lennon's assassin, is at Attica Correctional Facility in Attica, New York.

Manson disciple **Lynette "Squeaky" Fromme,** who is serving a life sentence for aiming a pistol at then-President Gerald Ford in 1975, is in Kentucky in the maximum-security wing of the Lexington Federal Correction Institution. She had fled from a women's prison in West Virginia at Christmastime in 1987 because she wanted to be closer to Manson during the holidays. She was moved from the West Virginia facility because she wouldn't promise a judge that she wouldn't try to escape again.

John Hinckley, the spoiled rich kid who took potshots at President Reagan to get actress Jodie Foster's attention, is in the locked mental ward at St. Elizabeth Hospital in Washington, D.C. (For directions see Nuts to You, page 112.)

Bank defrauder **Jake Butcher,** who headed the First United Bank of Tennessee, the bank that bankrolled the Knoxville World's Fair, is in Atlanta Correctional Institute.

Jean Harris, who murdered the "Scarsdale Diet" doctor, Dr. Herbert Tarnower, is serving fifteen-year-to-life prison term at the Bedford Hills, New York, prison for the 1980 shooting. She has written two books while in the slammer: the best-selling *Stranger in Two Worlds* and *They Always Call Us Ladies.*

James Earl Ray, convicted killer of Dr. Martin Luther King, Jr., is in Brushy Mountain State Prison at Petros, Tennessee, thirty miles west of Knoxville.

Joel Steinberg is serving eight to twenty-five years at the State Correctional Facility at Dannemora, New York, for his manslaughter conviction in connection with the death of Lisa, the six-year-old girl he and his girlfriend, Hedda Nussbaum, had raised without adopting.

Soul singer supreme **James Brown** is in Broad River Reception and Evaluation Center at 4460 Broad River Rd. in Columbia, South Carolina. (See also Shoot-Outs, page 227.)

The prisoner who changed a presidential election, **Willie Horton,** whose controversial prison furlough cost Michael Dukakis votes in the 1988 presidential election, was given a weekend furlough from Massachusetts Correctional Institute in Brockton to visit his family in Lawrence, Massachusetts. Horton, a convicted murderer, didn't return. Instead he headed south to Maryland, where he raped a woman. Dukakis, then Massachusetts governor, approved the furlough program that let Horton out. Horton is now in Maryland State Penitentiary in Baltimore serving two life sentences plus eighty-five years. He still owes Massachusetts the rest of his life sentence.

John Wayne Gacy, who was convicted of sexually abusing and killing thirty-three young men and boys and burying them in his basement, is in Illinois's Menard Corrections Center in Chester, Illinois. (See Mass Murder Sites, page 168.)

Arthur Bremer, who attempted to assassinate George Wallace in 1972 is in Maryland Correctional Institute in Hagerstown, Maryland.

Former PTL vice president **Richard Dortch,** who tried to save his own assets by pleading guilty to using PTL money for his own benefit, is serving an eight-year term at Eglin Air Force Base in Florida.

Country music star **Johnny Paycheck** is serving seven to nine-and-a-half years at the Chilicothe, Ohio, Correctional Institute for assault. Years earlier Paycheck had spent eighteen months in the Naval Disciplinary Command in Portsmouth, New Hampshire, for allegedly trying to help his commanding officer take his job and shove it.

Fatal Vision killer, **Jeffrey MacDonald,** is at Terminal Island prison in Long Beach, California.

☆ **Getting There:** Prisons are best viewed from the main road. Tourists aren't exactly welcome.

Lompoc Camp From Santa Maria, follow signs on Highway 20 from the airport. From Santa Barbara, take Highway 101 north to Highway 1; go through town and follow the signs.

Soledad Prison Take Highway 101 and follow the signs.

Corcoran Prison is at 4001 King Ave. in Corcoran, California. Take Highway 5 north. It turns into Highway 99; take Highway 43 exit at Tipton, which will bring you right into Corcoran. Exit on Whitley and make a left on King Avenue.

Attica Correctional Facility is in Attica, New York. From Highway 238 north, take Main St. into Attica. At the first light, take a left onto Exchange St. The facility is approximately one mile ahead.

Lexington Federal Correction Institution From Lexington, Kentucky, take US 421, Leestown Pike, north. The Federal Correction Institute is just past Masterson Station Park on the right.

Atlanta Correctional Institute From I-75-85 take University Ave. east. When it dead-ends into Ridge Ave.–McDonough Blvd., go right. It's just down the street.

Bedford Hills Prison From I-684 north toward Brewster, take Katonah exit (Exit 6); turn left onto Route 35. Take left at second traffic light onto Highway 117 south; follow to Harris Road. Prison is at 247 Harris Rd. It's about fifty miles north of New York City.

Brushy Mountain State Prison From I-40 take Exit 347 (Harriman) north to Wartburg (honest). It's about thirty miles. Go east nine miles on SR 62. Turn north on Petros Highway. It's about two miles.

Dannemora State Correctional Facility is in Dannemora, New York. From 87 north, take Exit 38N and go west on Route 374 for about fifteen miles; you can't miss it.

Broad River Reception and Evaluation Center is part of Broad River Correctional Institute. From Highway 26 east into Columbia, take second St. Andrews Rd. exit to Broad River Rd., where you'll take a left. Center is about one mile ahead on the right (4460 Broad River Rd.)

Maryland State Penitentiary in Baltimore is at 954 Forrest St. in Baltimore, Maryland. Take I-95 north to the Russell St. exit (downtown Baltimore); take Russell St. to Pratt St. Turn right on Pratt and go east (it's one-way). After about six blocks, Pratt St. widens. Get over to the extreme left. Two blocks later turn left on Gay St. (Gay St. is one-way also). Stay on the left-hand side of the street, and eight blocks later, make a left on Greenmount Ave. Go up to Eager St. and make a left; in the middle of the block you will see the entrance to the penitentiary.

Menard Corrections Center is in Chester, Illinois. Take Route 4 south from Centralia until you get to Route 150. Go south on Route 150 into Chester, and follow the signs.

Maryland Correctional Institute in Hagerstown, Maryland. From I-70 east, take Exit 29 (Sharpsburg); take left at bottom of ramp (Sharpsburg Pike). Go three miles on Sharpsburg Pike until you get to Rocksbury Rd.; take a left. Institute will be a quarter mile ahead on your right.

Eglin Air Force Base Prison In Pensacola, Florida, Take Interstate 10 to Highway 85 south, which will run into 189 south. Take 189 south to Eglin Blvd. Take Eglin Blvd. east and you'll run right into the main gate.

Chilicothe Correctional Institute is at 15802 State Road 104 in Chilicothe, Ohio. From I-23 to Chilicothe, take the Bridge St. exit. Follow Bridge St. all the way past the shopping malls and fast-food restaurants; make a right on Highway 35 (west). Take the first exit, which is High St. (State Road 104). Make a right at the light, and the prison is one mile ahead on the right-hand side.

Terminal Island Federal Correctional Institute is in California. From Los Angeles, take the Harbor Freeway south to the Vincent Thomas Bridge. Go across the bridge and make a left on Ferry St. Ferry St. will curve to the right and turn into Terminal Island Way; follow it through one light and two stop signs until it curves off to the left and becomes Seaside Way. Follow that street all the way out and you will come to the guard at the main gate.

PAST PRISON HOMES OF THE RICH AND FAMOUS

In the mid-seventies it was Little Washington at the Lewisburg Prison Camp, Lewisburg, Pennsylvania. Celebrity inhabitants included Watergate felons **Jeb Stuart Magruder** and **G. Gordon Liddy.** Bess Myerson's boyfriend **Andy Capasso** was in nearby Allenwood when Bess got in that sticky shoplifting situation. (See Sticky Fingers, page 32.)

John Ehrlichman, Nixon's advisor for domestic affairs, served his time at Swift Trail Federal Prison Camp in Stafford, Arizona.

John Mitchell, Nixon's Attorney General, was in jail at Maxwell Air Force Base in Montgomery, Alabama. **Charles Colson,** Nixon's special counsel, had spent seven months there in 1974.

Bob Haldeman, Nixon's White House chief of staff and Ehrlichman, the other half of the Nixon palace guard, served his time at Lompoc Camp, Lompoc, California. Nixon's dirty trickster **Donald Segretti** served four months at Lompoc. (For directions see page 185.)

Four of the Watergate burglars served their terms at Eglin Air Force Base minimum security camp in Florida: **Bernard Barker, Virgilio Gonzalez, Eugenio Martinez,** and **Frank Sturgis.** (For directions see opposite page.)

Subway Vigilante **Bernhard Goetz,** a former electronics engineer, worked in the radio shop at Rikers Island prison in New York.

Dan White, the so-called Twinkie Killer, who murdered San Francisco mayor George Moscone and alderman Harvey Milk, and then blamed it on his Twinkie addiction, was in Soledad Prison. He was later parolled, and in 1985 he committed suicide. (For directions see page 185.)

Robert Mitchum served forty-two days in the Los Angeles County Jail and at Wayside Honor Farm at Castaic in 1949 for possession of marijuana and conspiracy to violate the state's narcotics act.

Jerry Jeff Walker, the outlaw country music star, composed "Mr. Bojangles" in the New Orleans Jail where he was spending the night for unruly conduct.

Country music singer **Johnny Rodriguez** spent the night in the Bracketville, Texas, Jail for stealing three goats and barbecuing the evidence.

David Allen Coe, the Original Rhinestone Cowboy, spent four years in the Ohio State Penitentiary at Mansfield in the mid-sixties.

Merle Haggard's rap sheet is about as long as his discography. A joyride at eighteen landed him nine months in the Ventura County Jail. One of his scrapes with the law involved a drunken break-in at a Bakersfield bar and netted him two years nine months in San Quentin Prison in San Quentin, California.

Tex-Mex country star **Freddy Fender** spent three years in the Louisiana State Prison at Angola in the early sixties for possession of marijuana.

Ex-Congressman **John Jenrette** served two stints as a celebrity prisoner: his major stint was thirteen months in the Atlanta federal prison for the 1980 ABSCAM bribery probe. (He later spent fifteen days in jail in 1989 for stealing a pair of shoes from a department store in suburban Washington and altering prices on a pair of pants and a shirt. (See Sticky Fingers, page 34, for details.)

Gangster **Al Capone** served time in the Atlanta penitentiary for evading $215,000 in income tax. Atlanta prison also was home to Mafia informant **Joe Valachi,** socialist leader **Eugene V. Debs,** baseball player **Denny McClain,** Soviet spy **Rudolf Abel,** who was swapped for U-2 spy plane pilot Francis Gary Powers, and **Vincent Papa,** whose

Prison home of Al Capone—Atlanta penitentiary (photo by Chris Wohlwend).

case was the basis for the movie *The French Connection.* Debs, imprisoned for his opposition to World War I, ran his 1920 presidential campaign from his cell. He got more than one million votes.

Billy Sol Estes, Texas fat cat financier, served his time in the Big Spring Prison, Big Spring, Texas.

Religious skimmer **Rev. Sun Myung Moon** and radical priest **Father Daniel Berrigan** served time at the Danbury Prison Camp in Danbury, Connecticut.

Studio 54 bigwigs **Steve Rubell** and **Ian Schrager** served their tax-evasion terms at Maxwell Air Force Base in Montgomery, Alabama.

Mae West was sentenced to ten days on Welfare Island, New York, in 1926 after her Broadway play *Sex* was declared obscene. She only served eight days. Two days were lopped off for good behavior.

The Cisco Kid, Duncan Renaldo, spent eight months in the McNeil Island, Washington, prison in 1932 for illegally entering the United States from Mexico.

☆ **Getting There:** Here are the directions to the prisons.

Lewisburg Prison Camp is in Lewisburg, Pennsylvania. Take Interstate 80 to Lewisburg exit (Route 15 south). Take Route 15 south for eight miles until you get to Lewisburg. Go through one light and take a right at the second. As the road begins to curve off to the right, take a left on the road that is not marked. When you get to the stop sign (William Penn Dr.), take a right and follow that road to the Institute. When road construction around the prison is complete, you will need new directions.

Allenwood Prison is in Allenwood, Pennsylvania, and is next door to Lewisburg Prison.

Swift Trail Federal Prison Camp is in Stafford, Arizona. Take Highway 70 west to Highway 666. Go ten miles south on Highway 666 and the prison is on the right.

Maxwell Air Force Base Prison is in Montgomery, Alabama. Take 65 south to Montgomery; follow signs for Maxwell Air Force Base. Take a right at the second light and you'll see the guard for the base.

Rikers Island is the large island in the bay at LaGuardia Airport. From I-278 take the Thirty-first St. exit north. Go east on Ditmars Blvd. and then north on Hazen St. to the island. Call ahead. They don't cotton to pop-in company.

Los Angeles County Jail is in downtown LA at the corner of First St. and Hope Ave. From City Hall, take Main St. east to Sunset; take a right. Take Sunset to Vignes; make a left. From there you will see the jail.

Wayside Honor Farm is in Castaic, California. The Honor Farm is two miles north of Magic Mountain. Take Highway 5 to Hasley Cannon Rd.; follow Hasley Cannon Rd. to Old Rd. (at stop sign) and make a left. Then just follow the signs.

New Orleans Jail is at 730 South White St. Take I-10 into the city, exit at Orleans and make a left. Stay on Orleans until you get to Claiborne; make a right. Go straight on Claiborne until you get to Tulane. At the corner of Broad and Tulane, you will see the courthouse. Go one block past the courthouse (still on Tulane), and make a left at the first corner. Go as far as you can and you'll come to the jail.

Bracketville, Texas, Jail From San Antonio, take 90 west into Bracketville. Go past Rob's Mini-Store on the right. At a blinking light (next to Stop 'n' Shop) you will take a right. Go one block and you will see a hardware store on one corner and a bank on the other corner. The jail is right next to the bank.

Ohio State Penitentiary is at Mansfield. Take 71 North to Mansfield; exit Route 30. Take 30 east to Highway 545; you'll see the prison from Highway 545.

San Quentin Prison is in San Quentin, California. Go north on Highway 101 to San Francisco, cross the Golden Gate Bridge, and go past Cortemadera. At Larkspur Landing you will see a sign for the Richmond–San Rafael Bridge, start following that around to San Quentin.

Louisiana State Prison is in Angola. Take I-10 north toward Natchez, Mississippi. Get off at Baton Rouge going north on Highway 61. Pass through St. Francisville. Two miles later, take a left on Highway 66, and you'll see a sign for Angola. Follow that sign for twenty-one miles and you'll drive right up to the front gate of the prison.

Atlanta Federal Prison They're always working on the roads in Atlanta so any directions are contingent on the roads still being there. Just south of Atlanta Fulton County Stadium (home of America's team) from I-75-85 take Exit 89 east on University Ave. When it bangs head first into Ridge Ave.–McDonough Blvd., go right. It's just down the street on the right.

Big Spring Prison is in Big Spring, Texas. Take I-20 west; exit left at Highway 80. Take the feeder road west and take a left under the highway. Take the feeder road east, which is actually an extension of Highway 80. Go east on 80; when you get to the corner with a 7-Eleven on the left, take a right onto Airport Rd. Take Airport Rd. all the way to the entrance of the prison.

Danbury Prison Camp is in Danbury, Connecticut. From Stamford, take Route 7 north to Route 84. Go east on 84 to Exit 5, which is Route 37. Take 37 north three miles; institute will be on the right.

Welfare Island Prison is now called Roosevelt Island Prison. It is at 591 Main St., Roosevelt Island, New York. From

New York City, take the Roosevelt Island tram, which you can catch at Fifty-ninth St. and Second Ave.

McNeil Island Prison is at 1403 Commercial St. in Steilacoom, Washington. From I-5, take the Steilacoom–DuPont exit (Exit 119); turn right (there's a traffic light). Follow the winding road all the way to Steilacoom; it's several miles. When you get to a stop sign, straight ahead will be the bay. You'll see the McNeil Island Boat Dock. You have to ride a ferry across the bay to the island, and you need official permission to do it. So just look across the bay and say "Oh, Pancho" three times. That's tribute enough.

JOHNNY CASH'S PRISONS

Johnny Cash is so associated with prison that when you hear the name Johnny Cash, you immediately hear the song "Folsom Prison Blues" in your head.

And well it should be. The Man in Black has recorded two albums in prisons. In addition he has written and recorded a number of prison laments, including "I Got Stripes." All told he has recorded almost three hours of prison songs.

It would lead you to believe that Johnny has spent a lot of time in prison. Well, he has. Recording albums.

As for actual time in the slammer, Johnny has only an eight-hour stay in the El Paso jail for smuggling pep pills, a six-hour stay in the Starkville, Mississippi, jail for public drunkenness (he was picking flowers on the courthouse lawn at 2 A.M.), and another six-hour stay in the Lafayette, Georgia, jail for public intoxication.

But what an impact those twenty hours had on Cash. Whew!

☆ **Getting There:** To the El Paso jail: If you're going south on Mesa Blvd. (which is a main street downtown), take a left onto East Overland. Take a right on San Antonio, and you'll see the jail (a big, tall gray building), but you'll be facing the back of it. Since San Antonio St. is one-way, you'll have to make a circle to get around to the front.

To the Starkville jail: Take Highway 12 east to the intersection of Highway 12 and Highway 25. Go through the first three-way stop. At the next three-way stop, you'll see the police department.

To the Lafayette jail: Take 75 north to the Reseca-Lafayette exit; turn left. Go to the end of the road and turn right at the stop sign (onto Highway 136). Stay on 136 down a mountain; the road will stop and turn into 151 briefly; turn left on 151. Take the first right off of 151 to get back on 136. Take 136 through one light, and turn left at the second light. There you will see a big courthouse; the jail is behind it.

THE PERSONAL TOUCH

You can visit the Maine State Prison Store in Thomaston. It is staffed by an all-convict crew selling crafts made by inmates. Warning: shoplifters will be punished immediately.

☆ **Getting There:** From Portland, take 295 north to the Brunswick exit, which becomes Route 1. Take Route 1 north straight up the coast to Thomaston; prison will be on your right. The store is just beyond the prison.

PRISONCRAFTS

If you want to decorate your home in an all-prison motif, you can also buy handmade prisoner crafts at the Nevada State Prison Hobby Store and the San Quentin Prison Handicraft Shop in California.

The stock changes from week to week (as do the prisoners), but there is always a healthy supply of handmade wallets and belt buckles. Sorry, no ropes made from sheets or guns made in the metal shop.

☆ **Getting There:** The Nevada State Prison Hobby Store is at the corner of East Fifth and Edmonds in Carson City,

Nevada. The San Quentin Prison Handicraft Shop is on the east side of the prison at the main gate.

___

NO EXIT

If you want to see what prison is like, without actually having to don a pantyhose mask and stick up a convenience store, you can tour the most famous of them all, the escape-proof Alcatraz Prison, located on an island in the San Francisco Bay.

☆ **Getting There:** Never fear; Alcatraz is no longer a prison. The tour leaves from San Francisco's Pier 41, at Jefferson and Powell streets.

GANGLAND

—

They've been glamorized as modern-day Robin Hoods, but the only part that's true is the "hoods" part. They were just hoodlums out to make a buck and make a dame. But you don't have to be nice to make this book.

Make book? Make book? That has a familiar sound to it.

Here are some historic mobster spots.

DEAD DILLINGER

Manhattan Melodrama was playing on the big screen, but it was pure Chicago that happened outside afterward. Mobster John Dillinger was leaving the Biograph Theater on July 22, 1934, when he was gunned down by federal agents. He had been betrayed by the notorious Lady in Red.

☆ **Getting There:** The Biograph is still showing movies. It is at 2433 North Lincoln Ave. in Chicago. Dillinger was gunned down in the alley. Lincoln Ave. is US 41. The Biograph is north of the intersection of Lincoln and Fullerton, near De Paul University.

The other famous Dillinger story, the one about his remarkable organ being preserved in formaldehyde at the Smithsonian Institute, is, alas pure legend. The Smithsonian is at 1000 Jefferson Dr., NW, on the Washington Mall (that two-mile stretch of green between the Lincoln Memorial and the Capitol). And you can go ahead and ask anyway.

THE SCARFACE HOUSE

The most famous of all the mobsters of the thirties was Al Capone. The sixties TV series "The Untouchables" helped cement his reputation, so to speak, with a generation born too late to read of his deeds in the paper.

Although he spent much of his time at the Lexington Hotel, running his "business," Al Capone did have a home. And it's still there at 7244 South Prairie Ave. in Chicago.

Most of the other Capone crime spots are now parking lots. I like to think that's the way he would have wanted it.

☆ **Getting There:** From 1923 to 1932 Capone lived at 7244 South Prairie in a two-story red brick house. The Lexington Hotel was at Michigan and Cermak. The federal government recently approved a loan to convert the old building into a 258-suite business hotel. Prairie runs parallel to the Dan Ryan Expressway. The old Capone home is on Prairie between Seventy-second and Seventy-third streets.

When Capone shifted his operations to Cicero in 1924 his headquarters was the Hawthorne Hotel and Restaurant at 4823 Cermak Rd. Bugs Moran and his boys once sprayed the place with machine gun fire, trying to kill Scarface. Al survived by hiding under his bodyguard. It's now a parking lot, too.

Capone's Miami headquarters was at 10 Palm Avenue,

Palm Island between Miami and Miami Beach. The house is still there. (An airline pilot and his wife live in it.) Any of the myriad sight-seeing boats will point it out for you. Take 41-A1A (General MacArthur Causeway) from Miami to Miami Beach. Just past Watson Park on the left is Palm Island.

For a visit to his tomb, see Where Are They Now?, page 230.

WHERE SCARFACE GOT HIS SCAR

The way Al Capone told it, he was leading the troops in World War I when a bullet creased his cheek, leaving him with a permanent scar from his left earlobe to the curl of his lip. Great story but just that. Capone really got his scar during a barroom fight.

He was seventeen and working his way up the hood ladder by tending bar and bouncing drunks at Coney Island's Harvard Inn dance hall. When a stubby petty felon named Frank "Little Frankie" Galluccio came in with two babes, his girlfriend and his sister, Capone took a liking to Frankie's sister's posterior and told her as much. Little Frankie overheard and the posturing began. First it was words, then fists. It ended when Little Frankie pulled his penknife and sliced Capone's cheek twice. Al wanted revenge but was dissuaded by a rising young gangster named Charles "Lucky" Luciano. Eventually a mutual respect developed between Scarface and Little Frankie, and in later years, when Capone was a crime boss, he would hire Galluccio as his Brooklyn bodyguard.

☆ **Getting There:** The Harvard Inn was on Sea Side Walk on Coney Island.

ST. VALENTINE'S DAY MASSACRE

By modern standards it wasn't much of a massacre—only seven died—but because it involved gangsters and because it happened on February 14, it became famous as the St. Valentine's Day Massacre. The gangland killing occurred at SMC Cartage Company garage at 2122 North Clark Steet in Chicago in 1929. Gangsters disguised as policemen entered the building—it was where Bugs Moran stored his hootch—and ordered the seven Moran employees to line up against the wall. It was standard police procedure and the hoods did as they were told. By the time they figured out what was going on, it was too late. Capone, who had made himself very visible in Miami that day, said his men didn't do it. "The only man who kills like that is Bugs Moran." But shortly thereafter Capone checked himself into jail—for protection, was the rumor.

☆ **Getting There:** The building is gone. It's a vacant lot.

SAM, BAM, THANK YOU MAN

Chicago don Sam Giancana, the man the CIA hired to kill Castro, had been testifying before a Chicago grand jury investigating the mob. He hadn't told them anything, but there were rumors on the street that he was about to. Before he could make it back to court, he was gunned down in his Oak Park, Illinois, home. He was frying sausage, spinach, and beans in the kitchen at the time.

☆ **Getting There:** He lived in a modest home at 1147 South Wenonah Ave. in Oak Park. Get to Roosevelt Rd. in Oak Park (it's a main east-west highway). Wenonah intersects with it. Go north a block and a half.

WIPEOUTS

—

The causes of most traffic jams aren't traffic wrecks, they're rubbernecking drivers trying to get a good look at the wrecks.

Like gnats to a banana, we are drawn to wipeouts.

Here are some of the great ones.

REBEL WITHOUT A PULSE

It was "9/30/55," a day that has become so famous that director James Bridges named a movie (a bomb movie) after it. It was the day that actor James Dean wiped out at the Y intersection of Highway 46 and Highway 41 near Cholame, California. He rammed his Porsche into the side of a 1950 Ford Custom Deluxe Coupe that had pulled out in front of him.

Dean saw the eastbound car slowing at the intersection. His last words, to a passenger, were, "The guy's got to stop. He'll see us."

The driver of the Ford claimed not to have seen

Dean's car approaching. Probably not. Dean was estimated to be traveling in excess of 85 mph by troopers investigating the accident. He had received a speeding ticket for going 110 in a 35 mph zone just two hours earlier in Bakersfield. He was on his way to a race in Banning.

☆ **Getting There:** Cholame is twenty-five miles east of Paso Robles on SR 46. The crash site is opposite the post office, on the north side of Highway 46 and east of Maggie's Cafe. A small metal marker was erected on the site in 1987 by a Japanese businessman who now wants to put up a giant sculpture.

THE STREET CORNER WHERE MARGARET MITCHELL WAS RUN OVER

Margaret Mitchell, author of *Gone with the Wind,* may have been the most famous writer in America in August 1948, but she was also the most bored. She had spent the last several months in her Atlanta home, tending to her sick husband. By August 11, husband John Marsh seemed well enough that the two could go out together. They settled on an evening at the Peachtree Arts Theater, where *A Canterbury Tale* was playing. They parked on the other side of the street and were crossing when a Ford sedan driven by a drunken off-duty cabbie came careening down the street. Husband John scurried on across Peachtree Road but Margaret panicked and tried to retreat. The sedan, which police estimated was traveling 40 mph, ran over her. She died five days later in Grady Hospital. The driver, who had twenty-three prior traffic violations, was charged with involuntary manslaughter.

☆ **Getting There:** The Peachtree Arts Theater was downtown at the corner of Peachtree and Thirteenth streets. There's even a little plaque.

Where John Lennon and *Rosemary's Baby* were shot.

THE STORY OF JOHN AND YOKO

John Lennon and *Rosemary's Baby* were both shot at the Dakota. Mark David Chapman shot Lennon at the Seventy-second St. entrance.

☆ **Getting There:** The Dakota is at One West 72nd, right next to Central Park.

THE ALLMAN BROTHERS DISBAND

Guitar wizard Duane Allman had backed everyone from Wilson Pickett to Aretha Franklin when producer Phil

Walden talked him into forming his own band. He persuaded his brother Gregg among others, and the group began recording in 1969. It would be two years before the record-buying public would appreciate the hard-driving double guitar sound. And then, just as their album *At the Fillmore East* was climbing up the charts, Duane was killed in a motorcycle accident. He was riding down a Macon, Georgia, street on October 29, 1971, when it happened. This was just the first of many tragedies to beset the band. A year later bass player Berry Oakley was killed in a motorcycle crash only three blocks from the site of Duane's wreck.

The greatest tragedy the band encountered was when Gregg married Cher.

☆ **Getting There:** Duane was killed on the corner of Log Cabin Dr. and Hillcrest near Macon. Take Poplar or Mulberry north out of downtown (they both turn into Washington St.). Go over the interstate. Washington St. turns into Vineville Ave. About a mile and a half later take a right onto Pierce. Then make a right at the first light onto Hillcrest.

WHAT'S GOING ON?

It was just a little argument over an insurance policy, but before it was over, Marvin Gaye, satin-voiced singer of such hits as "I Heard it Through the Grapevine" and "Trouble Man," lay dead, killed by his father, Marvin Gay, Sr., a retired minister. (The younger Gaye had added the *e* to the end of his name when he started in show business.)

The forty-four-year-old Gaye had moved back in with his parents only months before, after the dissolution of his second marriage.

Gay, Sr., blamed the incident on his son's cocaine use, claiming Marvin, Jr., had turned into "something like a beastlike person."

Where Bat Masterson died: former home of the *Morning Telegraph*.

☆ **Getting There:** The Gay mansion where Marvin Gaye died is a large green and white Victorian with double gables. It is at 2101 South Gramercy Pl. in Los Angeles's Crenshaw neighborhood. Take the Western Ave. exit north from the Santa Monica Freeway. Go one block to Washington and west on Washington to Gramercy Pl.

BACK WHEN THE WEST WAS GETTING OLD

Legendary lawman of the Old West Bat Masterson didn't meet his demise at the OK Corral. Or any other gunfight for that matter. He didn't die with his boots on. He died with his brogans on. He keeled over at his desk at the New York *Morning Telegraph*, where he was sports editor. That's right, sports editor.

☆ **Getting There:** The *Morning Telegraph* was at 525 West 52nd St.

WON'T COME BACK

Just a year earlier they had had their biggest hit with a
song about a car crash involving drag-racing teens. Then
in late 1965 Jan Berry, half of the surfer duo Jan and Dean,
wiped out on the real Deadman's Curve. He suffered brain
damage and has spent the last quarter century recovering.
Three people were killed in the accident.

☆ **Getting There:** The real Deadman's Curve is on Sunset
Blvd. just west of Whittier Dr.

ON THE ROAD TO CALIFORNY

Alfalfa, the Little Rascal with freckles and a cowlick, had a
hard time making the transition to adult life after the end
of the *Our Gang* comedies. There just weren't many parts
for squeaky-voiced men. He was killed in 1959 in a dispute
over a dog.

Alfalfa had borrowed a hunting dog from welder Bud
Stiltz, and when the dog ran off, Alf had to spend $50 on
an ad and reward. He thought Stiltz should reimburse him.
Stiltz said Alf had borrowed the dog, Alf had lost the dog,
Alf had to pay to find the dog. Alfalfa got drunk and went
to Stiltz's house to demand the money. Alfalfa was arro-
gant. Stiltz was adamant. Alfalfa had a switchblade. Stiltz
had a gun. Alfalfa died in the ambulance on the way to the
hospital. It was ruled justifiable homicide.

☆ **Getting There:** From I-405 (San Diego Freeway) take
Devonshire east to Columbus (one block past Sepulveda).
Turn left (north) to 10400 Columbus Ave., a one-story tan
stucco ranch home. It's in the San Fernando Valley.

WHERE THIRTY-EIGHT WATCHED WHILE
KITTY GENOVESE SCREAMED

It is the most famous mugging murder in history. Entire
books have been written about it. Two generations of psy-

chology professors have scrounged up new majors with analyses of this event.

It is the infamous tale of the thirty-eight murder witnesses who didn't want to get involved.

Bar manager Kitty Genovese was returning home at 3 A.M. on the morning of March 13, 1964, walking from her red Fiat to her apartment half a block away when she was savagely attacked by Winston Moseley. She was stabbed twenty-six times during a half-hour period and repeatedly screamed, "Help me! He's killing me!" But not one of the thirty-eight residents who heard the screams did anything until it was too late. Moseley is serving a life sentence in the Green Haven Correctional Facility in Stormville, New York.

☆ **Getting There:** Kitty lived in an apartment in Kew Gardens on Austin St. in the New York City borough of Queens.

EVERBODY LOVES TO CHA CHA CHA

Sam Cooke died young. When the bullet from a .22-caliber pistol passed through his heart on December 11, 1964, he was only twenty-nine years old. He'd already had a string of silky-soul hits, "Chain Gang," "Another Saturday Night," "Only Sixteen," "Cupid," "Everybody Loves to Cha Cha Cha," "Twisting the Night Away." He'd influenced virtually every black musician of the time, but he hadn't enjoyed the commerical success that would certainly have been his when soul music sales took off in the mid-sixties.

On that December evening he and a twenty-two-year-old named Elisa Boyer checked into a $3-a-night room at the Hacienda Motel in south Los Angeles. They signed the register as Mr. and Mrs. Cooke. Sam was married at the time but not to Ms. Boyer. A few minutes later Boyer ran screaming from the room, tugging her clothes back on and carrying most of Sam's wardrobe. She would later testify that he began ripping at her clothes and she fled to call police. She didn't say exactly what she expected to happen when she checked into the motel with a married man.

Cooke, wearing a sports coat, one brogan shoe, and nothing else, stopped at the motel manager's door, thinking Elisa might be inside. When manager Bertha Franklin, fifty-five, refused to open the door, he pounded it down. Franklin then pumped three slugs into Cooke's charging body. When that didn't stop him, she pummeled him with a walking stick.

When police arrived moments later, Cooke was dead. His last words had been, "Lady, you shot me." The death was ruled justifiable homicide.

☆ **Getting There:** The Hacienda, now the Polaris Motel, was at 9137 South Figueroa in Los Angeles. Figueroa runs parallel to the Harbor Freeway (Interstate 110). Take Rosecrans Blvd. east to Figueroa and head south.

I'M SO LONESOME I COULD DIE

Where did country music legend Hank Williams, a.k.a. Hank Williams, Sr., die? He was found dead in the backseat of his pink 1953 Cadillac at a filling station outside Oak Hill, West Virginia, on January 1, 1953. He was on his way from Montgomery, Alabama, to Canton, Ohio, where he was to perform that night.

So where did he die? On the way he and his driver, Charles Carr, checked into the Andrew Johnson Hotel in Knoxville. He may have died there. He coughed when porters carried him to the car, but that could have been an involuntary reflex, and he might have already been dead.

Carr and the car were stopped near Blaine, Tennessee, at 11:45 P.M. on New Year's Eve for reckless driving. Carr was tried before justice of the peace O. H. Marshall in Rutledge at 12:30 A.M. Williams remained in the car.

☆ **Getting There:** From I-64-77 take US 19 to SR 16, which was US 19 in the fifties, into Oak Hill. Just north of the Herbert E. Jones Library, right in front of what is now

Blackburn Ford, is where Hank's driver stopped. Legend has it that it was at the Pure station (which is now a Union 76 station but looks like one of those little Pure stations of the fifties). But that's wrong according to the man who lives right next to the gas station and has for fifty years. He says he was there that night. "Not a great deal of excitement. You see I was in World War Two." And he says Hank died in front of the Ford dealership, which is right across the street from the hospital.

- The filling station in Oak Hill, West Virginia, which was Glen Burdette's Pure Oil Station, is now a Union 76 station.
- The Andrew Johnson Hotel in Knoxville is now the Andrew Johnson Office Building. It is on South Gay St. at the Tennessee River Bridge.
- Blaine, Tennessee, is on US 11W, "Bloody 11W" it was called then, the main road to Kingsport and Bristol.

Other sites from the life of Hank Williams:

- He married his third wife, Billie Jean Jones Eshlimar, nineteen, three times, twice before a paying audience at **Municipal Auditorium** in New Orleans (at the corner of North Rampart and Orleans streets). Both matinee and evening weddings were sold out at $1.50 a head. The weddings netted $30,000. Hank got so drunk that he missed the honeymoon to Cuba.
- His death car is in the **Hank Williams Jr. Museum** in Nashville. (See Where Are They Now?, page 231.)

IF YOU DON'T LIKE HANK WILLIAMS, GO FALL OFF A MOUNTAIN

And speaking of Hank Jr., or technically, writing of Hank Jr., the father's bad karma seemed to follow the son, too. Bocephus, as his father nicknamed him, nearly killed himself in 1975 when he fell off a cliff on Mount Ajax in Montana. He had just passed the nine-thousand-foot mark when he slipped and fell several hundred feet, landing face first on a boulder. It was not pretty and there's not much point in detailing all the damage.

☆ **Getting There:** I really can't direct you on a hiking trip. Mount Ajax is west of Dillon and south of Big Hole National Battlefield, near Jackson, Montana.

WHERE JFK WAS ASSASSINATED

The brouhaha over the museum at the Texas Book Depository in Dallas illustrates what this book is all about. Everyone knows what happened there. It's the most famous "Where were you when you heard . . ." question. But Dallasites were not happy to see the sixth floor, the assassin's lair of Lee Harvey Oswald, turned into a museum.

So instead of calling it the Assassin's Lair, or something equally tacky, they have gone in the completely opposite direction. It is called The Sixth Floor, a name so tasteful you might think the signs are advertising a trendy women's store.

The attraction is the lair, where Oswald set up his rifle. The attraction's promoters have arranged the book cartons just as Oswald had them set up. A clear plastic screen keeps you at gun's length from the exact spot, but you can look out any of the other windows and get pretty much the same view. Admission is $4. If you are a senior citizen, it is only $3.

☆ **Getting There:** The Texas Book Depository is in downtown Dallas at the intersection of Elm, Main, and Commerce.

You won't want to miss the Grassy Knoll, where the "second gunman" is supposed to have hidden. If you go behind the bushes and stand where the second gunman supposedly stood, behind the stockade fence, the first thing that will strike you is how close you are to the street

The Grassy Knoll—site of second gunman during JFK assassination.

and the spot where JFK was shot. If there were a second gunman and he missed—as the 1978 House of Representatives investigation concluded—then he had to be the worst shot in Western Civilization.

Oswald took bus 30, the Marsalis St. bus, from the Texas Book Depository two blocks before switching to a cab to go to his rooming house at 1026 Beckley St., where he was living under the assumed name O. H. Lee.

The rooming house is still there. In fact it's still a rooming house, and when we visited there was a sign out front "Rooms for Rent." The contents of Oswald's room have been removed and are set up just as he left them that day at the Tragedy in U.S. History Museum in St. Augustine, Florida (see Spare-Room Museums, page 162.)

Oswald was finally captured in the Texas Theater in the Oak Cliff neighborhood. (You remember the song: *John Wilkes Booth fled from a theater to a warehouse. Lee Harvey Oswald fled from a warehouse to a theater.*)

The Texas Theater is still a first-run movie house. When we visited, it was playing *See No Evil, Hear No Evil* with Richard Pryor and Gene Wilder. From the Dealey Plaza parking lot go right on Houston. Follow it around and over the viaduct—it becomes Zang—to Jefferson. Go right (west) on Jefferson one-half block to the Texas Theater. It's between Action Salvage and His Place contemporary Christian music, books, and gifts.

Coming back from Jefferson, turn right on Beckley. About a half-block up on the left is 1026, Lee's boarding house. It's a well-kept one-story brick home with cream-colored wrought-iron porch supports.

WHERE BOBBY KENNEDY WAS ASSASSINATED

Robert Kennedy had just won the California Democratic primary. He had just made a speech exhorting his followers to keep the momentum going and was walking through the kitchen of the Ambassador Hotel when Sirhan Sirhan stepped forward and shot him.

☆ **Getting There:** The Ambassador Hotel is at 3400 Wilshire Blvd. From the Santa Monica Freeway (I-10) take Western Ave. north to Wilshire. Go right. It's eight blocks down on the right.

WHERE MARTIN LUTHER KING WAS ASSASSINATED

Martin Luther King, Jr., was standing on the second-floor balcony of the Lorraine Motel in downtown Memphis when he was killed by a bullet from the rifle of James Earl Ray.

☆ **Getting There:** Ray was staying in a boarding house at 418½ South Main St. in Room 5B. He was paying $8.50 a week. As he escaped, he dropped his gun in front of 424 South Main, which was Canipe's Amusement Company. The Lorraine Motel is scheduled to become a museum. It's just around the block from Ray's rooming house. King and the Reverend Ralph Abernathy were staying in room 306. It was $13 a night.

WHERE NATALIE WOOD DROWNED

Natalie Wood drowned in 1981 off Santa Catalina Island when she slipped while boarding a small boat. She and husband Robert Wagner were on a boating outing that included Wood's co-star in *Brainstorm*, Christopher Walken. The circumstances are still mysterious although foul play isn't suspected, except by those who always suspect foul play.

☆ **Getting There:** Santa Catalina Island is twenty-six miles southwest of Los Angeles. That means it's out in the middle of the ocean. There are passenger ferries from Long Beach and San Pedro. Wood drowned in Isthmus Cove.

NUMBER ONE WITH A BULLET

Johnny Ace had six hit records before he was twenty-five. He had just recorded what he thought was his best song ever, "Pledging My Love," and was on a promotional tour to showcase the record. The Christmas Eve, 1954, stop was in Houston. Ace, the star of the show, was slated to go on last. He was backstage, showing off for the ladies, when he pulled a .22-caliber pistol from his pocket, stuck it in his mouth, and pulled the trigger. He must have known there was one bullet in the chamber but he had been so lucky so far in his career, he thought he could win at Russian Roulette, too. He died the next day. "Pledging My Love" went on to become number one on the Billboard Rhythm and Blues chart, a spot it held for ten weeks.

☆ **Getting There:** Ace shot himself backstage at the Houston City Auditorium, which was on the corner of Texas Ave. and Louisiana St. It's now a park.

SWEET DREAMS

They were three of the biggest stars of country music, Patsy Cline, Hawkshaw Hawkins, and Cowboy Copas. The trio had performed at a benefit show in Kansas City and were heading back to Nashville on March 6, 1963, when their plane crashed in a field three and a half miles west of Camden, a small town in west Tennessee.

☆ **Getting There:** From Memphis, take I-40 east to Exit 126. Take Highway 641 north to Camden. Once you get to Camden, take a left at the first light. Approximately two miles later, you'll see a landfill; take a right just in front of it. The plane crashed in a spot two miles down this road, about a thousand feet from the highway on the right.

SILKWOOD

Karen Silkwood was a disgruntled factory worker on her way to blow the whistle on her company for manufacturing defective plutonium rods when her small foreign car ran off the road and struck a concrete culvert. In death she became a symbol of the antinuclear forces, who say company goons ran her off the road.

Silkwood left the Hub Cafe in Crescent, Oklahoma, sometime between 7:15 and 7:30 P.M. on the night of November 13, 1974, heading for a meeting in Oklahoma City with a *New York Times* reporter. She had promised documents proving that her employer, the Kerr-McGee plutonium plant in Crescent, was poisoning its workers and acting irresponsibly in the manufacture of radioactive plutonium rods.

She never made her meeting. A half hour later she was found dead in her 1973 white Honda Civic. She had run off the left side of the roadway and crashed into a concrete ditch. Officers found strange dents on the left rear of her car, leading some to speculate that she was forced off the road. Her incriminating documents were never found.

☆ **Getting There:** Silkwood's car was found in the culvert on Route 74, exactly 7.3 miles from the Hub Cafe. She was to meet *Times* reporter David Burnham at the Northwest Holiday Inn in Oklahoma City. Her family eventually settled in a court suit against Kerr-McGee. They got $1.38 million, of which $810,000 went to pay attorney's fees.

KENT STATE: WHERE IT HAPPENED

In 1970 writer James Michener took time off from novelizing the histories of various obscure areas of the world to investigate the massacre of Kent State University students in Ohio. He concluded in his book *What Really Happened at Kent State?* that what really happened was the four students were shot dead by National Guardsmen. Sort of what we already knew.

☆ **Getting There:** The four students were killed in the parking lot in front of Taylor Hall and between Prentice Hall and the football field. The guardsmen fired from the area directly in front of Taylor Hall at the Pagoda.

WHERE RICK NELSON WAS KILLED

Ozzie and Harriet's boy Ricky Nelson was killed when the private plane he was riding in burned in a cow pasture near DeKalb, Texas, on December 31, 1985. He and his group, the Stone Canyon Band, had played their last show at P. J.'s Alley in Guntersville, Alabama, the night before.

☆ **Getting There:** Take I-30 east to Highway 259. Go north on Highway 259 to Highway 82. Go east to Highway 1840. Make a right on Highway 990, and the pasture you see on the far right-hand corner is the site of the plane crash.

WHERE JOHNNY HORTON WAS KILLED

Johnny Horton, who had the number-one hit of 1959 with "The Battle of New Orleans," was returning from a performance in Austin, Texas, to his home in Tyler when his white Cadillac slammed head-on into a Ford Ranchero.

☆ **Getting There:** Johnny Horton was killed on an overpass in Milano, Texas, on November 5, 1960. Take Highway 36 into Milano. Take a left at the light (Highway 79). About three hundred yards after you turn, you'll be on the overpass. (There will be railroad tracks beneath you.)

WHERE JAYNE MANSFIELD WAS KILLED

She was the poor man's Marilyn Monroe, so she had to try harder. Where Marilyn could pick and choose her roles, poor Jayne Mansfield had to take whatever would get her attention. And that included such embarrassments as *Dog Eat Dog, The Fat Spy, Hercules in the Vale of Woe,* and *Las Vegas Hillbillies.* It also included dinner theater. On June 29, 1967, she was on her way after appearing at Gus Stevens Dinner Club in Biloxi, Mississippi, to New Orleans where she was to appear on a TV show the next day. It was foggy, and in the murk her driver plowed their car into the back of a mosquito control truck. The top of her car was sliced off and Mansfield was decapitated. Also killed were the twenty-year-old driver, who had been supplied by the club, her boyfriend-manager, and her dog. Her three children were asleep in the backseat and survived.

☆ **Getting There:** In Mississippi take old Highway 90 and just before you get to the Rigollets Bridge, near a restaurant called the White Kitchen, is the spot. The people who directed me to the spot were more than anxious to remind me that Jayne wasn't just killed, she was decapitated. If you're having trouble finding the spot, ask a local; get the whole story.

HIGHER AND HIGHER

Jackie Wilson, famed soul singer whose hits ranged from "Lonely Teardrops" in 1958 to the classic "Higher and

Higher" a decade later, was performing in one of Dick
Clark's rock and roll revival shows at the Latin Casino in
Cherry Hill, New Jersey, in 1975 when he suffered a mas-
sive heart attack on stage. He suffered permanent brain
damage before he could be treated and spent the next ten
years in a stupor at a New Jersey nursing home. He finally
succumbed in January 1984.

☆ **Getting There:** The Latin Casino was at the present site
of Subaru of America, Route 70, Cherry Hill, across from
the Garden State Racetrack.

LANA'S GIRL

Lana Turner's daughter, Cheryl Crane, stabbed her mother's boyfriend, mobster Johnny Stompanato, to death in
1958. Mom and Johnny were arguing, and Johnny had just
threatened to cut Lana up into little pieces. So fourteen-
year-old Cheryl went to the kitchen, grabbed a nine-inch
butcher knife, and planted it in Johnny's heart.

☆ **Getting There:** It was at 730 North Bedford Ave. in Beverly Hills.

COULDN'T PUT HUEY TOGETHER AGAIN

Louisiana politician Huey Long was the inspiration for the
protagonist in Robert Penn Warren's epic novel *All the
King's Men*. Long was the hero of the common man, but,
unfortunately for him, not all common men. On September
8, 1935, the Kingfish, as he was called, was just outside the
governor's office in Baton Rouge when a disgruntled voter
shot him. The assassin, twenty-nine-year-old eye-ear-nose-
and-throat specialist Dr. Carl Weiss, Jr., was unhappy because his father-in-law would have been gerrymandered
out of a judgeship by a bill Long was pushing. Long stumbled across the rotunda and down twenty-eight steps before collapsing. He died two days later.

☆ **Getting There:** The governor's office is on the first floor in the state capitol building at 900 Riverside in downtown Baton Rouge. In the hallway just outside the governor's office there are four recessed marble pillars. Weiss was behind the pillar nearest the chamber where the House met. Huey was moving toward a group of men standing on the circular design in the center of the floor when Weiss moved toward him and fired. Huey, who was mortally wounded, ran west down the corridor toward the Senate for forty feet, then turned into the passageway to the stairs. He stumbled down the twenty-eight steps to the basement. He was taken out the rear door and put in a passenger car, which delivered him to Our Lady of the Lake Sanitorium a quarter mile away down Third St.

ANCHOR'S AWAY

NBC anchorwoman Jessica Savitch was already on the downhill slide on October 20, 1983. Only three weeks earlier, she had appeared drunk when she read the headlines during a prime-time newsbreak. The episode was given wide media coverage and many whispered that it was a drug problem. She and date Martin Fischbein, a *New York Post* vice president, drowned when he made a wrong turn when leaving a restaurant parking lot and drove into a rain-swollen canal.

☆ **Getting There:** They had just dined at Chez Odette in New Hope, Pennsylvania. It is on South River Rd. Fischbein drove to the back of the parking lot, turned north onto a towpath, ignoring two signs that read "Motor Vehicles Prohibited." He swerved left and the car flipped over, landing upside down in the Delaware Canal mud, which sealed the doors. From Philadelphia, take I-95 north to the New Hope–Yardley exit. Make a left on Taylorsville Rd., and another left on Route 32. Five miles later, you'll see the restaurant on the right-hand side. For reservations call (215) 862-2432.

WHERE BUDDY HOLLY, RITCHIE VALENS, AND THE BIG BOPPER WENT TO ROCK AND ROLL HEAVEN

You know about this: you've seen the scene in *The Buddy Holly Story* and later in *La Bamba*. (When is someone going to make a movie about the Big Bopper?)

1959. The Winter Dance Party, a bus tour of one-night stands featuring rockers Buddy Holly, Ritchie Valens and J. P. Richardson (the Big Bopper). They were tired. They were cold. They weren't through with the tour. So Holly chartered a plane to take them from Clear Lake, Iowa, to their next date in Moorhead, Minnesota. The exact flight was from the Mason City, Iowa, airport to the Fargo, North Dakota, airport, the airport nearest Moorhead.

In the wee hours of the morning on February 3, 1959, the four-passenger Beechcraft Bonanza carrying the three and pilot Roger Peterson crashed in a pasture on Albert Juhl's farm.

☆ **Getting There:** The Mason City airport is at Exit 197 on I-35. The plane crashed eight miles north.

WHERE FIREBALL ROBERTS WIPED OUT

At some barbershops they talk politics. At others, baseball, football, basketball. When I was a kid, I got my hair cut at a stock-car barbershop. All the conversations were about stock-car racing. And the arguments they would get in . . . all over who was the best, Junior Johnson or Fireball Roberts. (This was before Richard Petty was a factor on the stock-car racing circuit.)

Roberts ended those discussions when he wiped out during the World 600 race in 1964. He died on July 2, 1964, from injuries sustained a month earlier in an accident during the race.

☆ **Getting There:** The wreck was at the Charlotte Motor Speedway in Charlotte, North Carolina. It's on Highway 29 north in Concord, North Carolina, about twelve miles northeast of Charlotte. You can take a bus tour of the speedway that includes a lap of the track. The phone number for tour information is (704) 455-2121.

A MOVIE TO DIE FOR

It was, at best, a mediocre movie, a feeble attempt at re-creating the magic of the original TV show. But *Twilight Zone—The Movie* has come to symbolize even more.

Three actors—Vic Morrow and two small children—were killed during the filming of the first episode. Director John Landis escaped punishment after a jury trial, and then invited the jurors who acquitted him to a movie premiere.

Only in Hollywood.

☆ **Getting There:** A helicopter crashed during filming, decapitating Morrow and squashing the two Vietnamese children. The scene was filmed at Indian Dunes motorcycle park in Velencia, California, north of Los Angeles. The park is at 28700 Henry Mayo Dr. From the Golden State Freeway (I-5) just north of Magic Mountain and Six Flags, take Henry Mayo Dr. west to the park.

The title of a book about the incident and the subsequent trial tells it all: *Outrageous Conduct*.

IT BRINGS ON MANY CHANGES

Suicide is an occupational hazard in Hollywood. It can also be a career boost, but only if you leave something behind to boost.

Here are some celebrity suicide sites:

Comedian **Freddie Prinze** shot himself to death in 1977 in his home at 865-75 Comstock Avenue in Westwood.

☆ **Getting There:** From Wilshire Blvd. turn north on Comstock.

The nation was shocked in 1969 when the media reported that **Diane Linkletter,** daughter of friendly talk-show host Art Linkletter, had taken LSD and leaped to her death from the sixth floor of an apartment building. She made her leap from the shabby building at 8787 Shoreham Drive in West Hollywood.

☆ **Getting There:** On Sunset Blvd., just west of Sunset Plaza, turn right on Horn and then right on Shoreham.

George Reeves, the star of the Superman TV series, which showed in the fifties, died mysteriously in his Benedict Canyon home in 1959. His girlfriend answered the door and told the visitor George was going to kill himself. Seconds later there was a gunshot. And sure enough ol' George was dead on the bedroom floor, under very mysterious circumstances.

☆ **Getting There:** Reeves lived at 1579 Benedict Canyon Rd. From Sunset Blvd. turn north on Benedict Canyon Rd.

THE OLD MAN AND THE KEY

Hemingway committed suicide at his Idaho home by putting a shotgun to his forehead and pulling the trigger. His wife had been concerned about his recent bout of depression and had locked his guns up. But he knew where to find the keys.

☆ **Getting There:** It's in the Sawtooth Mountains near Sun Valley, Idaho. Take Highway 75 north from Sun Valley. Just before you get to Saddle Road (near the Big Wood Golf Course), look to the left. His home is just north of the Presbyterian Church.

CELEBRITY OD'S

With a gun, it's pretty apparent it was suicide. But sometimes it's impossible to determine if the celebrity intended to do himself or herself in. Was that drug overdose intended to bring an intense high or the ultimate low?

Here are a few celebrity OD spots:

Janis Joplin OD'd in the Landmark Motel at 7047 Franklin Avenue in Hollywood in 1970. The Landmark Hotel is now the Highland Gardens.

Nick Adams, the Rebel, OD'd in his home at 2126 El Roble Lane, Beverly Hills, in 1968.

"Sick" comedian **Lenny Bruce** was found dead of an overdose of morphine in 1966. The needle was still in his arm. Bruce died in his home at 8825 Hollywood Boulevard.

"Saturday Night Live" star **John Belushi** died of an OD in a bungalow at Chateau Marmont in 1982. From Sunset Boulevard take Marmont Lane north around the hotel. Turn right on Monteel. Go past a brush area and a carport. You'll see two bungalows, B-3 and B-4. Belushi was in B-3.

SHOOT-OUTS

What is it those bumper stickers say? OUTLAW GUNS AND ONLY OUTLAWS WILL HAVE GUNS? Heaven forbid that the outlaws get any more guns. Look at what they've already done . . . .

THE SUBWAY VIGILANTE'S SUBWAY

The New York tabloid headline writers, bless their pica poles, nicknamed him the Subway Vigilante. Bernhard Goetz, a nerdish engineer, shot four youths who approached him on a New York subway car in 1984.

Goetz claimed the young men were trying to rob him. They insisted they were just asking to borrow money. And surrounding him while they did it.

He beat the attempted murder rap but was sentenced to a year in prison for illegally possessing a firearm.

☆ **Getting There:** Goetz and the young men had their tussle on the Seventh Ave. No. 2 line subway.

DO AS I SAY OR I'LL SHOOT YOU

"There should be a complete and universal federal ban on the sale, manufacture, importation, and possession of handguns," liberal political columnist Carl Rowan wrote in his syndicated column in October 1985.

Three years later, in the early morning hours of June 14, 1988, Rowan heard noises outside his expensive Washington-area home. He found an unregistered handgun in his drawer, went outside, and shot a teenage prankster who was frolicking in his pool and Jacuzzi.

At his trial for possession of an unlicensed handgun, Rowan claimed the eighteen-year-old intruder threatened him. Rowan, sixty-three, also testified he thought the revolver was exempt because it was given to him by his son, an ex-FBI agent and federal marshal.

☆ **Getting There:** Carl Rowan's home is in the 3100 block of Fessenden St. NW., Washington, D.C. The pool and Jacuzzi are in back.

JODIE! HEY JODIE! LOOK AT THIS!

On March 30, 1981, spoiled rich kid John Hinckley, unable to get actress Jodie Foster's attention any other way, decided to prove his love to her by firing a round of bullets at the president. One shot hit President Reagan, another disabled press secretary James Brady, and a third injured FBI agent Raymond Martin. The other shots burrowed into the pavement.

☆ **Getting There:** Reagan was exiting the Washington Hilton (1919 Connecticut Ave. NW, Washington, D.C.) by the Nineteenth St. door.

GEORGE WALLACE WAS HERE

George Wallace, the Alabama redneck, has played a large part in national politics. Who can ever forget his stirring

Laurel Shopping Center: where George Wallace was shot.

speech on the steps of the University of Alabama, something about preferring a "barbed-wire enema" to integration? Of course the black students were enrolled that day anyway.

Had Wallace not entered the 1968 presidential campaign as an Independent, siphoning off much of the Southern Democrat vote, Hubert Humphrey might have won the election and Watergate would be just a hotel.

Wallace's political career, and very nearly his life, came to an end on May 15, 1972, in the parking lot of a Laurel, Maryland, shopping center. Loner Arthur Bremer, who had been trailing Wallace for weeks, got the candidate's attention by yelling, "Hey George! Come over here! Come over here!" When Wallace stepped that way, Bremer began firing away.

☆ **Getting There:** Wallace blocked the door to Foster Auditorium on the campus of the University of Alabama in Tuscaloosa.

Laurel Shopping Center.

Laurel Shopping Center is at 14828 Baltimore-Washington Blvd. Take the Baltimore-Washington Parkway toward Baltimore. Exit on Highway 197 and bear left when it splits. Take a left at the first light (you'll see a 7-Eleven); you'll still be on Highway 197. Stay on that until you get to Cherry Lane.; make a left. Stay on Cherry Lane until you get to Route 1; the shopping center will be at the intersection of Cherry Lane and Route 1.

ON THE ROAD WITH JAMES BROWN

In 1988 Papa got a brand-new set of legal problems.

It was a hard year for the "hardest-working man in show business." During that period the Godfather of Soul, as Brown is also known, and his missus were arrested eight times on charges ranging from possession of illegal drugs to assaulting a police officer.

Let's go on the road with James and Adrienne Brown:

First Stop We begin our tour at Browns' Beech Island, South Carolina, home, a sixty-two-acre spread across the Savannah River from Augusta. It's not hard to find. Their green-and-brown ranch house sits at the end of a private drive marked by a sign that reads "James Brown Boulevard." Do not drive up the driveway.

On April 3, 1988, Adrienne called police to the house and charged that her husband, high on the hallucinogenic drug PCP, beat her with a metal mop handle and then fired four shots into her Lincoln Town Car while she was sitting in it. She told *People* magazine, "He had taken my Black Diamond mink—this is my $35,000 coat—laid it outside on the ground, and he shot at it."

Next Stop Bush Field, Augusta, Georgia, which is two miles south of I-540 on SR 56. The next Saturday, April 9, Adrienne was arrested at the airport and charged with possession of PCP.

Next Stop Sheraton-Wayfarer Motor Inn at the junction of routes 3 and 101, Bedford, New Hampshire. One month later, on May 9, Adrienne was charged with possession of PCP and setting fire to the Browns' hotel room. James told police, "She threw a cup of coffee at me."

Next Stop Nine days later, on May 18, James led Aiken County police on a high-speed car chase along Route 278 after they were called to his home to settle a domestic dispute. Police charged him with assaulting an officer and possession of PCP, and the court sentenced him to perform a benefit concert. To retrace the chase take US 278 from Beech Island, South Carolina, to US 1-78.

Back To Bush Field, Augusta, Georgia. On May 20 police stopped Adrienne as she arrived on a flight and found two canisters of PCP hidden in her bra. She claimed "diplomatic immunity" because her husband was once declared an "international good-will ambassador." Her lawyer later withdrew that claim.

Next Stop Richmond County Jail at 401 Walton Way in Augusta.

Adrienne was jailed on June 15 for failing to appear at her arraignment on drug charges. She was behind bars for five days before James, on a European tour, found out and arranged bail.

On the Road with James James crashed an insurance seminar in the building where he has an office on September 24, brandishing a shotgun and demanding to know who had been using his rest room. Police were called and James led them on a half-hour chase. He ran a roadblock and had his front tires shot out, and then doubled back into Georgia driving on the rims. The chase ended in a ditch in Augusta. Police testified he was incoherent when they finally caught him. "He was pouring sweat like he'd come out of a swimming pool," said Sergeant Frank Tiller of the Richmond County Sheriff's Department. "He was obviously under the influence of something stronger than alcohol."

Police said that as he was being booked, he broke into his "good foot" dance.

☆ Getting There:

Starting Point James Brown Enterprises Office, Executive Park at 1056 Claussen Rd., Augusta, Georgia. (Exit I-20 at Washington Rd. Go west. Claussen Rd. is right there: it runs parallel to I-20.)

Head to Washington Rd. At the corner of Washington and Claussen is where officer Larry Overstreet unsuccessfully tried to stop Brown. Hop onto Interstate 20 and head east toward South Carolina. Officer Overstreet abandoned the chase at the state line. Brown continued on to North Augusta. Get off the interstate at Martinstown Rd. and head south. It was at the intersection of Martinstown and Gordon Highway where officers began to set up a roadblock. Brown ignored the blockade and aimed his truck at the two officers who were trying to stop him. They shot out his front tires, but Brown continued driving on the rims onto Gordon Highway, (US 1-78). Head back south to Augusta, then turn east on Broad St., go sixteen blocks, and take a left on Courtland Dr. It dead-ends into Fairhope St., where Brown ran the truck into a ditch.

He was taken to the Augusta-Richmond County Law Enforcement Center at 3500 Deans Bridge Rd. and booked on several misdemeanor charges and then taken to the

Aiken County Detention Center at 1455 Georgia Ave. in
North Augusta, where he was booked on two counts of
assault and battery with intent to kill and several lesser
charges.

Brown spent the night of September 24 here. The next
day he was arrested for DUI.

Next Stop Aiken Civic Center, Aiken, South Carolina.
Brown staged his court-ordered benefit October 22 in this
arena. The event started with wrestling matches and continued with music from members of Lynyrd Skynyrd, the
Atlanta Rhythm Section, and other bands, and concluded
with James, who performed "I Feel Good," one verse of
"Papa's Got a Brand New Bag," and then said good-bye in
three languages before beating a hasty retreat. Only 381
customers paid, leaving 7,119 empty seats.

Next Stop Aiken County Circuit Court, 109 Park Ave.,
Aiken, South Carolina.

In December 1988 James Brown was tried, convicted,
and ordered to serve six years of hard time.

Final Stop Broad River Reception and Evaluation Center
at 4460 Broad River Rd. in Columbia, South Carolina. (For
directions see Celebrity Hard Time, page 186.)

James began serving a six-year sentence on December
19, 1988. A number of prominent musicians came to his
aid with the song "Free James Brown." His earliest probation is 1991.

WHERE ARE THEY NOW?

—

Once they were famous. Now they are . . . well . . . where are they?

SUNNY VON BULOW'S CURRENT RESIDENCE

Utilities heiress Martha "Sunny" von Bulow, America's most famous vegetable since they pulled the plug on Karen Ann Quinlan, has been wasting away in her private room in an Upper West Side hospital since an insulin overdose sent her into a coma in 1980. She is still attended by private nurses who change the flowers in the room daily and play opera music through a Walkman.

Sunny became a famous comatose when husband Claus von Bulow was convicted in 1982 of trying to kill her with insulin injections. His conviction was later overturned, and at a 1985 retrial he was acquitted.

Sunny and Claus were divorced in 1988, after he signed an agreement with his stepchildren giving up all rights to his wife's $50-million estate in return for the reinstatement of the inheritance rights of his and Sunny's only child, daughter Cosima. He also promised not to write a book about the family. He has since moved back to Europe.

☆ **Getting There:** Columbia-Presbyterian Hospital is at 622 West 168th St. in New York City.

Sidetrip Sunny and Claus's former home is the seaside mansion on Millionaire's Row in Newport, Rhode Island, known as Clarendon Court. The three-story mansion was also the setting for another famous high-society soap opera, the 1956 film *High Society*, which starred Grace Kelly, Bing Crosby, and Frank Sinatra.

Another Side Trip On the walls of the great stairway in the Metropolitan Museum of Art in New York City, plaques bearing the names of major contributors to the museum can be found. On the north wall the names of Sunny and Claus are etched forever together in stone.

I'LL HAVE THE LUNCH SPECIAL
WITH CEMENT SHOES ON THE SIDE

Jimmy Hoffa, the fiery ex-president of the Teamsters Union, went to lunch on July 30, 1975, and never returned. He is presumed dead, presumed killed by Mafia figures hired to prevent his return to the Teamsters Union.

The chief suspect is Anthony "Tony Pro" Provenzano, former boss of the northern New Jersey Teamsters. They had some run-ins at Lewisburg penitentiary. According to the book *Desperate Bargain: Why Jimmy Hoffa Had to Die*, by Lester Velie, during one prison yard argument Pro had yelled at Jimmy, "I'll tear your heart out." They ran into each other at an airport a few years later and began fighting. Hoffa broke a bottle over Pro's head.

Hoffa's body has never been found, but it is supposedly in Pine Barrens Nature Preserve in the New Jersey wetlands. There have also been rumors for years that Hoffa lies in the concrete surface under the playing field of the Meadowlands Sports Complex in East Rutherford, New

Jersey. *Playboy* reported in 1989 that he's near the west end zone in front of section 107.

☆ **Getting There:** He was last seen at Machus Red Fox restaurant at 6676 Telegraph Rd., which is US 24, in Birmingham, Michigan, north of Detroit. Hoffa had driven his green Pontiac down from his summer home in Lake Orion, Michigan, nineteen miles away. The restaurant is the on the west side of Telegraph, south of Maple, right in front of the Bloomfield Shopping Center. From I-75 take the Fourteen Mile Rd. exit west to Telegraph. Then turn right.

Pine Barrens is an enormous area in southern New Jersey. If you want to look for the body, start at Wharton State Park. From the Garden State Parkway take SR 542 west thirteen miles to Batsto.

SIX FEET FROM FAME

John Belushi: Abel's Hill Cemetery, Chilmark, Martha's Vineyard, Massachusetts.

Karen Carpenter: Forest Lawn Memorial Park, Glendale, California (1712 Glendale Ave.)

Andy Gibb: Forest Lawn, in Glendale, California.

Billy Carter: Lebanon Cemetery, Plains, Georgia.

Larry Fine (Larry of the Three Stooges): Forest Lawn, in Glendale, California.

Al Capone: Mount Carmel Cemetery (corner of Wolf Road and Harrison) in Hillside, Illinois, a Chicago suburb. His old monument (his body was moved) is at Block 52, Mount Olivet Cemetery, 2755 West 111th Street.

Mae West: Row EE of the Cypress Hills Cemetery mausoleum, 833 Jamaica Avenue, Brooklyn.

Gummo Marx: Forest Lawn, in Glendale, California.

Carl "Alfalfa" Switzer: Hollywood Memorial Park (6000 Santa Monica Boulevard) Hollywood, California.

Sharon Tate: Holy Cross Cemetery (5835 West Slauson Ave.) in Culver City, California.

Zasu Pitts: Holy Cross Cemetery, in Culver City, California.

Freddie Prinze, Forest Lawn–Burbank (6300 Forest Lawn Drive) in Burbank, California.

Marilyn Monroe, Westwood Memorial Park (1218 Glendon Avenue) in Westwood, California.

DEAD CELEBRITY CARS AND CELEBRITY DEATH CARS

There's no thrill like the thrill of sitting behind the wheel where Elvis once sat. Or Hank sat. Or Hank died.

To get your kicks on Route 66:

- The car **Hank Williams** died in, a pink 1953 Cadillac, is in the Hank Williams Jr. Museum at 1524 Demonbreun in Nashville.

- The convertible **Jayne Mansfield** was riding in when she was decapitated in 1967 is in the Tragedy in U.S. History Museum in St. Augustine, Fla. (For directions see Spare-Room Museums, page 163.)

- The 1944 Cord that cowboy star **Tom Mix** was driving when his suitcase came untied and flew forward, breaking his neck and killing him instantly, is in the Tom Mix Museum at 721 North Delaware in Dewey, Oklahoma.

- **Bonnie and Clyde,** that delightful couple made famous by Warren Beatty and Faye Dunaway, took America by storm, literally, in the thirties, as they drove across the country, living off the fat of the land and the money in the small-town banks. They robbed banks and killed people. And became heroes in 1967 with the romanticized movie version of their lives. Bonnie and Clyde's real death car is at Whiskey Pete's, a casino-hotel at the California-Nevada line on I-15. The real Bonnie and Clyde didn't die in slow motion. Their death car from the movie is at the Tragedy in U.S. History Museum. Bonnie is buried in Crown Hill Memorial Park in Dallas. Clyde is in the West Dallas Cemetery.

- The **Buford Pusser** death car, the one the legendary *Walking Tall* sheriff was driving when he was ambushed and killed, is in the Carbo Police Museum in downtown Gatlinburg, Tennessee.

And if you think sitting behind the same wheel as Elvis is a thrill, you should try actually tooling along in a dead celebrity's car.

National Car Rental in Los Angeles has a fleet of classic cars that at one time included the late **Karen Carpenter**'s red-and-tan 1962 Chrysler 300, the late **Chet Huntley**'s blue 1955 Cadillac, and the late **David Janssen**'s 1960 Cadillac.

One customer who rented the Karen Carpenter car reported turning on the radio and hearing a Karen Carpenter song. (At this point pretend you can hear the theme music from "The Twilight Zone.")

The problem is these cars wear out and have to be replaced so I can't tell you what will be available when this book is published. National can tell you though.

You have to be a member of National's Emerald Club to rent one of these classics. To join call a National rental agent for an application.

The cars are available only at the LA airport and must be returned there. The phone number is (213) 670-4950.

☆ **Getting to the LA Airport:** If coming from the south, exit San Diego Highway at Imperial Highway and go west. Turn right on Sepulveda Blvd. and that will take you to the airport loop. From the north take Lincoln Blvd. to Sepulveda.

"Dynasty" fans can rent **Krystle Carrington**'s blue Rolls-Royce or **Alexis**'s white Rolls Silver Spur at Luxury Rent a Car on Wilshire Blvd., in Beverly Hills. The company has other cars with movie and music industry connections. Ask. Wheedle if you must; they are cagey about it.

☆ **Getting There:** Call (213) 657-2800 for reservations.

DEAD DOGS

—

Man's best friend, they call him. Just ask Richard Nixon. A dog salvaged his political career. Here are the graves of a few Great Dogs, and a few other Great Pets in American History.

CHECKER'S GRAVE

He is the most famous dog in political history: the dog who saved Richard Nixon's political career. In the late summer of 1952 Nixon, the vice presidential candidate on the Republican ticket, was under fire for using money from a slush fund set up by GOP fat cats. Nixon went on the defensive, speaking to the nation on the infant information system, television. He whined, he complained, he tried to blame someone else, and then he pulled up the family's pet, a cocker spaniel named Checkers. "Checkers here was a gift to my little daughter Tricia from a lobbyist in Washington and we aren't going to give him back." The maudlin sentimentality of the plea somehow got Nixon off.

☆ **GETTING THERE:** Checkers is buried in the Bide-a-Wee Association Pet Cemetery at Memorial Park. It's at 3300 Beltagh Ave., Wantagh, Long Island, New York. The phone number is (516) 785-6153. There are burials daily at 10, 10:30, 11, and 11:30 A.M. and 1, 1:30, 2, 2:30, and 3 P.M. From the Southern State Parkway take exit 28 south to Wantagh Ave. Bear right and go to the fifth traffic light to Beltagh Ave. Go right. The cemetery is opposite Wantagh High School. Checkers is buried in plot 5.

THE RASCALS' DOG

His real name was Jiggs, but to the generations of kids who loved the "Little Rascals" movie shorts, he was Petey, the rascal dog with the black circle around his eye.

☆ **Getting There:** When Jiggs died of old age in 1947, his owners buried him at the Aspen Hill Pet Cemetery, 13630 Georgia Ave., Silver Springs, Maryland. The phone number is (301) 871-6700. From the Capital Beltway, exit at Georgia Ave., which is 97 north. Take 97 north to Aspen Hill Rd., where you make a left. Then take another quick left (it's almost like a U-turn) into the driveway of the cemetery. Also buried there are Herbert Hoover's dogs and Rags, the dog who saved numerous lives during World War II.

THEM RASCAL DOGS

On September 6, 1986, as *Air Force One* circled overhead, two neighborhood dogs chose the runway of the Topeka airport to consummate their friendship. Security officers, unable to uncouple the pair, decided they were a security risk and shot them. President Reagan's plane then landed without incident.

☆ **Getting There:** Forbes Field, where the President landed, is south of town, just east of US 75 at SE Fifty-third St.

Forbes Field has two intersecting runways, which run northeast to southwest and northwest to southeast. In the quadrant nearest Highway 75 you will see a number of taxiways. One runs north and south. The dogs were coupling at the intersection of that taxiway and one that angles into it from the southeast. An investigation by journalist Alexander Cockburn later revealed that the dogs were shot nearly an hour after the Reagan plan landed. So the dogs died in vain.

OLD TROOPE

In the South a good coon dog is as important as a good wife. Maybe more important. When his favorite blue tick coon dog, Old Troope, passed away in the night in 1937, following a successful hunt, Key Underwood erected a memorial to the dog and opened Coon Dog Memorial Park. This happy hunting ground for coon dogs is now the final resting place for more than a hundred beloved old hounds.

☆ **Getting There:** Key Underwood Coon Dog Memorial Park is near Cherokee, Alabama. From Cherokee go about twelve miles south on Colbert County Rd., State Route 21.

NOT FRESH HORSES

Hopalong Cassidy's horse Topper, Tonto's horse Scout, and twenty-seven thousand other pets are laid to rest at the SPCA Pet Memorial Park in Calabasas, California.

☆ **Getting There:** From Highway 101 (Ventura Freeway) take Calabasas Parkway north. Turn right on Ventura Blvd. and left on Old Scandia. It's at 5068 North Old Scandia Lane.

THE GATE OF HEAVEN

The pet cemetery to end all pet cemeteries, so to speak, is the Bubbling Well Pet Memorial Park in Petaluma, California. This was the subject of Errol Morris's acclaimed — and hilarious—documentary *Gates of Heaven.*

☆ **Getting There:** It's at 2462 Atlas Peak Rd. From Highway 121 turn toward Silverado Country Club.

———

THE NUTTY PUPPIES

Jerry Lewis's dead dogs, ten of them, along with hundreds of other deceased pets, are interred at Pet Haven Cemetery-Crematory in Los Angeles. There's no indication if the French think the dogs were geniuses.

☆ **Getting There:** It's at 18300 South Figueroa St., where it intersects with 189th St. Exit the Harbor Freeway (I-110) at Carson St. Go right to South Figueroa and left about twenty-eight blocks. Or plot your own route if you don't like that one. From downtown LA, go south on the Harbor Freeway about fifteen minutes. Other famous owners whose late pets are buried here include Ike and Tina Turner, Nat "King" Cole, Ava Gardner, Alan Ladd, Groucho Marx, and Jaclyn Smith (who recently buried her second pet here).

WHAT A FRIEND WE HAVE IN JESUS

The eighties were not kind to the chosen, those ministers whom God had selected to go on TV for him. But as the church signboard said, "Jimmy Swaggart isn't supposed to be perfect; God is."

THE THEME PARK THAT JESUS BUILT

Religious fervor led the ancient Egyptians to erect the Sphinx. The same for the Druids and Stonehenge. But as best we can determine there is only one theme park in the world built as a monument to Christianity: Heritage USA, erected by PTL televangelist Jim Bakker.

☆ **Getting There:** Heritage USA theme park is in Fort Mill, South Carolina.

From I-77 take Carowinds Blvd. Go south on Carowinds Blvd. until you come to a fork in the road; when you do, bear left. That will take you to Heritage Village Blvd. . . . and you're there. Jerry Falwell took a ride down the water slide.

REPENT! THE END IS NEAR!

During the PTL trials (and tribulations) comedian Jay Leno pointed out that "Jim Bakker has been warning about Judgment Day for years. When it finally comes, where is he? Hiding under a desk."

☆ **Getting There:** In the middle of his fraud trial, Bakker was found curled in the fetal position under his attorney's desk. The address of attorney Harold Bender's office is 200 North McDowell St. in Charlotte, North Carolina.

OH, HOW THE MIGHTY DO FALL

Tammy Bakker operated the new ministry she and Jim started from a storefront in Shopper's World, a rundown, out-of-the-way strip mall in Orlando's factory outlet district. It was called the New Covenant Church, and it shared the mall with the Oriental Bazaar, the Designer Boutique, and two bars. Tammy moved the church to parts unknown after she fell behind in the rent.

☆ **Getting There:** Shopper's World is located at 6303 Grand National Dr. in Orlando, Florida. Go west on I-4 toward Disney World (south of Orlando), and get off at Kirkman Rd. (Kirkman is one of those rare exits that goes off to the left.) Take a left on International Dr. and then another left on Grand National Dr. The mall will be off on its own.

PEOPLE'S TEMPLE

It all started here.

It ended in the jungles of Guyana with the mass suicide of more than nine hundred believers.

It was Jim Jones's People's Temple, the Indianapolis church that became more than a religious headquarters, evolving, along with the personality of leader Jones, into a cult that demanded absolute obedience.

☆ **Getting There:** The original People's Temple was at 1502 North New Jersey St. in Indianapolis. Jones moved his congregation to San Francisco in 1971.

THE TERROR OF TINY EVANGELISTS

When the school year began in Marion, North Carolina, in the fall of 1987 so too did the school yard ministry of eleven-year-old Duffy Strode. The pint-sized preacher accosted his fellow grade-schoolers with warnings about "whoremongers" and "fornicators." He was suspended for disrupting school. When he returned, he renewed his ministry. And the school administration renewed his suspension. After his seven-year-old sister, Pepper, and his six-year-old brother, Matthew, joined him in preaching, they too were suspended. The Strode Family ministers are now taught at home by their father, David.

☆ **Getting There:** Eastfield Elementary School is at 711 Yancy St. in Marion, North Carolina. From I-40 take Highway 226 north into Marion. At the light just north of the Kentucky Fried Chicken, take a right onto Baldwin Ave. Go to Clark St. and make a right. When you get to the end of the street, take another right. Half a block later is the entrance to the school.

FEAR AND LOATHING IN THE PULPIT

He was a minister without a pulpit. Dr. Hunter S. Thompson was a doctor of divinity and an ordained minister in the Church of New Truth, a mail-order religion. But mostly he was a writer, head of the national affairs desk for *Rolling Stone* magazine. Thompson was known as the inventor and chief practitioner of "gonzo journalism," a now-extinct writing form best described as search-and-destroy journalism written in the first person, with emphasis on drug consumption and the resultant vomiting.

While covering Super Bowl VIII (1974) in Houston for

Rolling Stone, Thompson found his pulpit. He delivered a stirring sermon to the assembled multitude in the lobby of the Houston Hyatt Regency, about fourteen drunken sportswriters.

His sermon was based on Revelation 20:15, a quote he found in a religious tract: "And whosoever was not found written in the book of life was cast into the lake of fire."

☆ **Getting There:** Thompson delivered his sermon from the twentieth-floor balcony of the Hyatt Regency in Houston. It is at 1200 Louisiana St. downtown, just east of I-45, at the corner of Pease and Louisiana.

CROSS-SHAPED HOME

Harrison Mayes devoted all his life and most of his fortune to erecting concrete roadside crosses warning motorists to "Prepare to Meet God" and promising "Jesus Is Coming Soon." If you went to Florida in the fifties, you saw them.

He began his cross ministry after a near-fatal coal-mining accident. While in a coma, he saw a vision of a giant cross and vowed to spend the rest of his life erecting these religious symbols. He even built his home in the shape of a cross. Many of the crosses have crumbled and fallen or been mowed down as highways were widened. The house still stands. Mayes died about three years ago.

☆ **Getting There:** The house is at 409 Chester Ave. in Middlesboro, Kentucky. In Middlesboro from US 25E take KY 74 west toward downtown. Go under the underpass and turn left on Chester Ave. The house is tan. The "If You Go to Hell It's Your Own Fault" sign out front has been taken down. But there are still crosses in the backyard.

WERE YOU THERE WHEN THEY PHOTOGRAPHED MY LORD?

———

We all know what Jesus looks like, right? We've seen the pictures.

Same thing for his mother, Mary.

And even though it's been almost two thousand years since he walked the earth, some of his followers are still seeing his countenance in the most unlikely places: in food, in the sky, on rusting tanks and fading signs.

Mary's image, too.

REFRIGERATOR JESUS

Arlene Gardner, who lives close to Nashville had had it with her refrigerator. It was time to get a new one. But as southerners are wont to do, she put the busted one on the front porch rather than send it to the dump. Then one night she noticed some neighbors out front of her trailer, gawking.

It's Jesus, they told her, squinting their eyes and cranking their heads as they stared at her old refrigerator.

She walked the seven steps out to the road and took a look for herself, and she agreed. The light from neighbor Katherine Partin's front porch bulb created an unmistakable image on her old refrigerator: a bearded profile.

Willie Nelson, a few argued. But Arlene was adamant. It was Jesus. It had been foretold in one of her dreams.

Soon two thousand people were driving past her trailer every night. Most saw Jesus. Some thought maybe it was Willie. A few saw nothing.

Bob Mankin of nearby Tullahoma was sure it wasn't Jesus. "When the good Lord comes, he won't come on a major appliance," he told a reporter.

☆ **Getting There:** Arlene Gardner lives on Spring Creek Rd. in Estill Springs, Tennessee. Her neighbor has pulled the plug so you might not be able to see Jesus just now. But Gardner is trying to figure out a place to move the refrigerator so his countenance can return.

From Nashville, take Highway 24 south to Manchester and Highway 55 to Tullahoma. Make a left on Highway 41 and go seven miles; make a left on Spring Creek Rd.

Mrs. Gardner asks that you call first before coming. The number is (615) 649-5788.

OIL TANK JESUS

Rita Ratchen was driving home late one evening in 1986 from a job installing drapes when the oil tank on the side of Ohio Route 12 grabbed her attention. "Oh my Lord, my God!" she screamed. Her car nearly left the road as she stared at the image on the tank containing soybean oil. It was Jesus ministering to a small child.

☆ **Getting There:** The image was on the last tank in the Archer Daniels Midland Company lot on SR 12, about one mile west of Fostoria, Ohio. It has since been painted over, so the image is no longer visible, but if you squint . . .

NINE-HUNDRED FOOT JESUS

On May 25, 1980, at exactly 7 P.M. Oral Roberts, the original televangelist, saw a nine-hundred-foot tall Jesus towering over his Oklahoma religious base, the City of Faith. Roberts told reporters, "He reached down, put His hand under the City of Faith, lifted it, and said to me, 'See how easy it is for me to lift it?' "

Roberts didn't explain why he didn't tell anybody about this vision for a full five months.

Seven years later, on January 4, 1987, Roberts announced his latest vision: God had called him in and told him he would "call him home" if he didn't raise $8 million by March 31. Roberts said he had felt "death on me" two or three times during a ten-day vigil in the tower of his Tulsa, Oklahoma, office.

Viewers responded to God's blackmail threat and swamped Roberts with $9.1 million in contributions.

☆ **Getting There:** The Prayer Tower of Oral Roberts University is in southeast Tulsa, Oklahoma. From I-44 take Lewis Ave. (Exit 227) south to the campus. You'll see it. Jesus was three hundred feet taller than the tower.

Sidetrip US District Court at 339 Court Ave. in New Orleans. Douglas Coggeshall filed a suit in US District Court against Oral Roberts for portraying God as a blackmailer. He asked Roberts to return all donations.

MARY IN THE SKY

A vision of the Virgin Mary appeared to many in a crowd of twelve thousand gathered in Lubbock, Texas, in 1988 in hopes of seeing the mother of Jesus. The pilgrims were gathered in response to messages parishioners at St. John Neumann Catholic Church said they had received from the Virgin Mary, raising hopes of a miracle during the feast of the Assumption of Mary into heaven.

When sunlight broke through the clouds at 6:10 P.M.

on the evening of August 15, 1988, many reported seeing the Virgin Mary. When church pastor Monsignor Joseph James began to sing "Amazing Grace," one woman got up from her wheelchair. The crowd shrieked, "She walks, she walks." However the woman said later she could walk but was in the wheelchair for another ailment.

☆ **Getting There:** St. John Neumann Catholic Church is at 5802 Twenty-second St. in Lubbock, Texas.

THE SHRINE OF THE DISCARDED CRUTCH

They come from all over, seeking the healing powers of the Santuario de Chimayo shrine near Los Alamos, New Mexico. And from the number of crutches and braces on the walls, they must find them.

But the Amazing Randi, a magician who specializes in debunking "mysteries," says it is not positive proof that the cures have taken place. Then what happens to all the people who leave their prosthetic devices there? He investigated and reported: "The answer is that they simply fall down." He says the crutches and braces change from time to time because orthopedic surgeons and others must reclaim the devices left by poor patients who can't afford to replace them.

☆ **Getting There:** The Santuario de Chimayo shrine is located about twenty miles east of Los Alamos in Chimayo. It's on the east end of town. Take SR 76 east from SR 68.

SLEEPING JESUS

The eyes of the statue of Jesus at the Holy Trinity Roman Catholic Church in Ambridge, Pennsylvania, were once open, but during a Good Friday service parishioners reported the eyes closed. They now go back and forth, sometimes they seem open, other times closed. And the once-vivid color now seems to be sweating.

☆ **Getting There:** Ambridge is on SR 65 northwest of Pittsburgh. The church is at 415 Melrose Ave.

WEEPING MARY

A painting of the Virgin Mary at St. Nicholas Albanian Orthodox Church in Chicago appeared to parishioners to be crying in 1986.

☆ **Getting There:** The church is at 2701 Narraganset Ave.

UNRECOGNIZED SHRINES

—

It's hard to believe, but did you know that in Los Angeles they don't have a plaque at the site where Richard Berry wrote the words to "Louie, Louie?" But they do have a star on Hollywood Boulevard for Wayne Newton. Talk about misplaced priorities.

This chapter focuses on sites the locals don't know about or don't care about or both.

—

HE DIED SO THAT WE WOULDN'T HAVE TO JOG

Runner Jim Fixx, the author of the best-selling running book of all time, made the world safe for all us nonexercisers when he collapsed and died while jogging on a remote Vermont road in 1984. His death by jogging gave us just the omen we needed: "See," we would say, "see what happened to him. You won't catch me jogging."

☆ **Getting There:** Fixx collapsed fifty feet north of the Village Motel on US Route 15 in Hardwick, Vermont. From Burlington take SR 15 to Hardwick. It's about fifty miles.

BIRTHPLACE OF DUCT TAPE

My wife says her father holds his life together with duct tape. He uses the wide, gray stuff for every household repair job you could imagine and a few you couldn't. He's not the only one.

Duct tape is more than just tape, it is a way of life.

Among the ingenious uses found for it over the years:

- Beauty contestants use it to give their breasts the right lift.
- Rock music roadies hold their spider's nest of mike and speaker wires together with it.
- Stock-car racers use it to hold stray parts onto their cars and to streamline cracks.
- Police officers have been known to use it to bind prisoners, and kidnappers have been known to use it to tie up their victims.
- Teenagers repair old shoes with it. Old men repair torn upholstery. Concrete workers use it instead of gloves.
- It works as a roach trap, a luggage label, and a sailor's friend. America's Cup captain Dennis Conner used it to tie down riggings and lines and even to eliminate friction on the boat's hull.
- In the summer of 1976 Harold Brown of Rockville, Maryland, used it to close a two-inch gash in his left leg, caused when a wedge flew out of a log he was splitting.
- In the summer of 1988 Dan Smeragliuolo of Baltimore used it to repair a radiator leak in the truck that was transporting him and his bride through the Masai Mara game preserve in Kenya during their honeymoon.
- Ashland Oil Company workers used it in 1988 to repair a leaking gasoline tank.
- And Michael Dukakis's son John used it to hold his father's hands firm to the podium during an important

New Hampshire speech so the candidate wouldn't move them around so much.

You should salute this modern miracle product by visiting its birthplace in Secaucus, New Jersey.

Duct tape was invented in 1930 at the Johnson & Johnson factory in East Windsor, New Jersey. It was first known as Drybak, a white waterproof cloth tape developed for use in hospitals. During World War II it was modified to hold together ammunition boxes. But it didn't acquire its modern name and distinctive gray color until after the war, when air-conditioning took off, and sealing ducts became an important occupation.

There are three major manufacturers: Nashua Tape Products of Watervliet, New York, Polyken Technologies of Westwood, Massachusetts, and Shuford Mills, Inc., of Stony Point, North Carolina. Combined they turn out about 250 million square yards of duct tape a year. Enough to completely cover Manhattan. With enough left over to fix your shoe.

☆ **Getting There:** The only duct tape manufacturer that offers a factory tour is Shuford Mills on Route 90 in Stony Point, North Carolina. You must call in advance to arrange a tour. The number to call is (704) 332-2700. If you just want to pay your respects by driving by, take the Taylorsville exit from I-40. Go ten miles north on Route 90. The factory is on the left.

The birthplace is at Johnson & Johnson Dental Products, 20 Lake Dr., in East Windsor, New Jersey. From the New Jersey Turnpike take Exit 8 west to East Windsor (that sounds weird, but it's correct). Lake Dr. runs north of SR 571. Sorry, no tours.

HOME OF VELCRO

This amazing fastening material has almost as many uses as duct tape:

- It is used by astronauts to told tables and chairs in place in zero gravity so they will have a sense of up and down. It was also used on the space shuttle to keep the orbiter device from floating around the cabin.

- Elementary school kids prefer sneakers with Velcro fasteners.
- The army uses Velcro fasteners in uniforms.
- Special Blessings dolls, the first dolls that believe in a divine being, can kneel and stick their hands together in prayer because of Velcro pads.
- The Revenger, a battery-powered device that goes on your dashboard and emits machine gun, grenade launcher, or death-ray noises attaches with Velcro.
- David Letterman once dressed up in a Velcro suit and hurled himself onto a Velcro wall. He stuck.

Velcro was created in 1948 by a Swiss engineer who noticed that burrs stuck to his socks. The US manufacturing rights are owned by Velcro U.S.A. in New Hampshire.

☆ **Getting There:** Velcro U.S.A. is at 406 Brown Ave. in Manchester, New Hampshire. From I-293 take Exit 2, which is Brown Rd. Go north twelve blocks. It is on the right. Sorry, no tours.

HOME OF THE EDSEL

Call it what you will, the Ugliest Car Ever Built, the Biggest Flop in Automotive History, the Worst Car of 1958 (which *Consumer Reports* did). Most of the 109,466 Edsels built between July 1957 and November 1959, when Ford threw in the towel and discontinued the line, were built at Louisville's Ford assembly plant on Fern Valley Road.

The name Edsel has come to be synonymous with failure, flop, turkey.

When the International Edsel Club had its convention in Louisville in 1972, the theme was "Edsel Comes Home."

Now go see the home.

☆ **Getting There:** The Ford plant is at 3232 Fern Valley Rd. in Louisville, Kentucky. From I-65 take Fern Valley Rd. west. And there it is.

WHERE EVEL KNIEVEL BROKE EVERY BONE IN HIS BODY

Not really. Even Evel admits now that he never broke as many bones in his career as a daredevil (he prefers to call it "professional risk taker") as others claimed.

Still he did quite a job on himself when he attempted to leap his motorcycle across thirty-six cars in the Houston Astrodome on March 23, 1972. He cleared thirty-five cars, clipped the thirty-sixth with his front tire, went head-over-heels into the ramp, and was taken by ambulance to the hospital. A hospital spokesman at the time said, he had broken ninety-three bones. Knievel now says he broke only thirty-five in his entire career. Whatever.

☆ **Getting There:** The Houston Astrodome is at I-610 and Kirby Dr.

TARNISHED GUT

He was the Man with the Golden Gut. He could watch a TV series pilot and instantly divine its fate: schedule it here, change that, rewrite that. Freddie Silverman had been the program chief at CBS and ABC, so when he took over NBC in 1978 everyone expected miracles. What they got was "Pink Lady and Jeff." And other embarrassing TV shows. Soon he was fired.

But in those few months before his golden gut began to fail him we read a lot about Freddie's past successes. And we also read about his fabled masters thesis, the one that landed him a network job straight out of college. You can read for yourself what the once and future king predicted about television from his vantage point in the fifties. It's not all that impressive.

☆ **Getting There:** The Fabled Thesis is in the Ohio State University library on campus in Columbus, Ohio.

I ONLY READ THE ARTICLES

What Lewis and Clark did for the great Northwest, Masters & Johnson did for sex. They explored every inch of it, so to speak, researching and writing and making it a safe topic for dining room discussions. What would Ward Cleaver think if he were alive today.

☆ **Getting There:** The fabled Masters & Johnson sex clinic is at 24 South Kingshighway Blvd. in St. Louis, Missouri. There's a Kingshighway exit on I-70.

IS IT ILLUSTRATED?

Before Masters and before Johnson and before Masters & Johnson, there was the Kinsey Report, the pioneering 1948 sex study that revealed such shocking facts as: we like sex.

☆ **Getting There:** The Kinsey Institute is on the campus of Indiana University in Bloomington, Indiana. Ask. Anyone can direct you.

WHERE RICHARD BERRY WROTE THE WORDS TO "LOUIE, LOUIE"

Almost forgot. Richard Berry wrote the words to "Louie, Louie" on toilet paper while waiting backstage at the Harmony Club Ballroom in Huntingdon Park.

☆ **Getting There:** The ballroom was at 2409 West Slauson in Huntington Park. From the Harbor Freeway (I-110) take Slauson east.

UNLIKELY EVENTS

———

Sometimes it seems as if I'm living in a dream world. Like the night I fell asleep with the radio on and woke up to hear that former President Reagan was recovering nicely from . . . from . . . from what?!

And that led to this chapter about unlikely events.

———

WHERE REAGAN HAD BRAIN SURGERY

Taking one out or putting one in?

☆ **Getting There:** It was at the Mayo Clinic in Rochester, Minnesota. From I-90 take US 63 north to Rochester. It becomes Broadway. Go left on Second St. SW.

———

WHERE JERRY LEE LEWIS WENT TO BIBLE COLLEGE

Just before he turned fifteen Jerry Lee was sent to Southwestern Bible Institute in Waxahacie, Texas, to try and straighten him out. He returned home a few weeks later, expelled for playing "My God Is Real" boogie-woogie style. As he left he told the administration, "You can't get the Bible from all these silly books y'all got here."

☆ **Getting There:** Southwestern Bible Institute is at 1200 Sycamore St. in Waxahacie, Texas. From Dallas, take 35 south through DeSoto. About ten minutes later, take Exit 77 and follow the signs for Waxahacie. Go all the way through town (under a bridge, past a McDonald's on the right and a high school on the left). Turn right at Sycamore St. (you'll see a big green sign for the Institute), and go all the way to the end of the street.

WHERE DONNA RICE WAS A PHI BETA KAPPA

The playmate of presidential hopeful Gary Hart, Donna Rice, was a magna cum laude graduate of the University of South Carolina and holder of a Phi Beta Kappa key.

☆ **Getting There:** The University of South Carolina is in Columbia. It's the biggest dot on the South Carolina map. You can find it. From I-126 take the University exit and follow the signs.

WHERE BARRY MANILOW STUDIED MUSIC

The Sovereign of Schmaltz, Barry Manilow, actually studied classical (i.e., "good") music at the world-renowned Juilliard School in New York.

☆ **Getting There:** Juilliard is in Lincoln Center Plaza in New York City.

WHERE MICHAEL JORDAN COULDN'T MAKE THE BASKETBALL TEAM

In an era when Bobby Knight is scouting eighth-graders, it seems unbelievable that Michael Jordan, the most exciting basketball player ever, couldn't make his high school varsity. But it's true, as the *Enquirer* says. Jordan didn't make the varsity basketball team at Laney Emsley High School (Wilmington, North Carolina) until he was a junior.

☆ **Getting There:** Laney Emsley High is on N.C. 132 Highway. From Wilmington take US 74-76 to SR 132.

WHERE BEACH BOY DENNIS WILSON DROWNED

He was the only member of the seminal sixties surf-rock band, the Beach Boys, who could surf. So who would have thought that drummer Dennis Wilson would drown. It happened on December 28, 1983, in an empty slip at Marina Del Ray, California. He had been diving for junk at the bottom of the bay. And maybe drinking too.

☆ **Getting There:** Wilson drowned near the Via Del Mar Marina on Marqueas Way. From the Santa Monica Freeway take Lincoln Blvd. south to Washington St. Go right and follow it to Via Marina. Take a left. Marqueas is the third left.

WHERE MIKE TYSON RECEIVED A PH.D.

In 1989 Central State University in Wilberforce, Ohio, awarded high school dropout and heavyweight beating champion, Mike Tyson, an honorary Ph.D. in humane letters. Presumably for his ring work with Michael Spinks, et al.

☆ **Getting There:** From I-70 take Exit 54 (SR 72) into Clifton and follow the signs.

WHERE OLD MILWAUKEE BEER IS BREWED

Uh, it's not in old Milwaukee. Old Milwaukee beer is brewed in Longview, Texas; Van Nuys, California; Memphis, Tennessee; St. Paul, Minnesota; and Winston-Salem, North Carolina, but not in Milwaukee, Wisconsin. You can visit any of the five Old Milwaukee breweries, just don't forget and go to Milwaukee.

TOTAL WEIRDNESS

S ome tourist sights defy categorization. They fit only into the Chapter of Total Weirdness. In other words, I couldn't figure out how to fit them in any other chapter so here they are . . .

PUTTING THE "P" IN PRESIDENT

You're driving south on I-83, the Jones Falls Expressway through Baltimore. You take a quick glance to your right at the statue of George Washington. Then you snap your head back for the double take. You scream: is he doing what I think he's doing? No, he isn't, but it sure looks like it.

If you glimpse the statue from a certain angle, it appears that the Father of our Country is taking a whiz.

☆ **Getting There:** Look east as you approach downtown heading south. Wait until you are parallel with the statue.

MAN'S FATTEST FRIEND

The world's fattest dog is a 310-lb. Saint Bernard named Joshua, owned by Thomas and Anne Irwin of Grand Rapids, Michigan.

☆ **Getting There:** Joshua and his owners live at 5136 Cascade Rd. in Grand Rapids, Michigan. Visitors are welcome but *by appointment only*. Phone ahead: (616) 949-0560. If you're coming into Grand Rapids on 96 west, take Exit 40B, which is Cascade Rd. (You can only go right.) The Irwin residence will be about one and a quarter miles down the road, across from St. Matthew's Church.

WORKING STIFF

You don't have to go to Egypt to see a mummy. You can go to Paducah, Kentucky, instead. There at Hamock's Mortuary is the mummified remains of Speedy Atkins, a black handyman who died in 1928. They keep him in a closet.

☆ **Getting There:** Hamock's Mortuary is at 427 South 7th in Paducah.

WHERE THEY TRIED, CONVICTED, AND HANGED AN ELEPHANT

We're not talking primitive society here. Well, maybe. We're talking Erwin, Tennessee, a small mountain community in east Tennessee. On September 13, 1916, the townsfolk here charged a rogue elephant with murder, convicted her, and hanged her.

The elephant in question, a circus performer named Five Ton Mary, had turned on an inexperienced handler when the Sparks Circus was playing in nearby Kingsport. Walter Ethridge was riding on her back when she spotted a watermelon rind. She was heading for the treat when he jerked on her head with a spear-tipped stick. She reached around with her trunk, grabbed him, and threw him into a soft drink stand, then went over and stepped on his head.

Mary was arrested the next day after the circus had moved to Erwin. Officials walked her to the Clinchfield railroad yards, tied a seven-eighths-inch chain around her neck and hanged her with a 100-ton derrick.

☆ **Getting There:** From US 19-23 take SR 81 south to Main St. Go right. Turn right on Opekiska St. It dead-ends into the railroad shops where the elephant was hanged.

"NO SHOW" JONES

After Elvis's concerts, the Colonel would have the announcer tell the crowd, "Elvis has left the building" to get the fans to clear the premises.

At George Jones's concerts, on the other hand, it got to the point where they had to announce that he'd entered the place.

Jones may be the finest country singer alive, but what good is that whiskey voice if you can't hear it. Over the years George has had a serious problem with showing up for his scheduled concerts. In 1977 and 1978 alone he missed fifty shows. It got so serious that he acquired the unaffectionate nickname: George "No Show" Jones.

In fact in 1982 songwriters Glenn and George Martin penned a tune for Jones and Merle Haggard called "No Show Jones." Jones, of course, missed the recording session and Haggard recorded it alone. It's on their duet album.

Here is a tour of some of the fine arenas where George didn't show over the years:

- The Exit/Inn at 2208 Elliston Pl. in Nashville scheduled a "Nashville Loves George Jones Night" for December 5, 1980. He didn't show.
- In February 1977 he slipped out of a bathroom window at New York City's Bottom Line, 15 West 4th St., missing a star-studded show that CBS Records had

arranged to showcase his talents. Left waiting in the audience were Walter Cronkite, John Chancellor, and the president of CBS Records. It was the first of several times he failed to show at the Bottom Line. (He finally made a show there on August 18, 1980.)

- In 1977 he rescheduled a performance at Phoenix's Veteran's Memorial Coliseum (1826 West McDowell) for the next night, then failed to show then, too.

- In 1978 he missed two shows in Richmond, Virginia, and a court later awarded the two promoters $29,654 in a default judgment. George failed to show for the hearing.

- Between 1978 and 1982 he missed five scheduled shows at the Pequea Silver Mines Club in Lancaster, Pennsylvania.

- In February 1981, he no-showed at the Ohio Theatre (14 West 17th St.) in Columbus.

- In the spring of 1981 he failed to show at Kings Island amusement park near Cincinnati, Ohio, prompting a $10.1-million lawsuit by the promoter.

- Later that year he missed a show at Kiwanis Park in Wichita Falls, Texas.

- He sneaked out of a backstage dressing room at the Grand Ole Opry in October 1981, missing a show for four thousand industry folks gathered for CBS Records' Country Music Week artists' showcase. (The Grand Ole Opry House is on the grounds of Opryland.)

- A few days later he failed to show for a concert at the Salem-Roanoke Civic Center in Salem, Virginia.

- On January 10, 1982, he failed to show for a concert at the Lambuth College Coliseum in Jackson, Tennessee.

- On May 1, 1982, he didn't show for a concert at Florence-Lauderdale Coliseum in his hometown, Florence, Alabama.

- In August 1982 he didn't show for a concert at Coffee County Auditorium in Tullahoma, Tennessee.
- Later that same month he didn't show for a concert at the Ector County Coliseum in Odessa, Texas.
- In Denver in 1982 he didn't show for a concert at McNichols Arena (1635 Clay St.) even though his manager had posted a $2,000 guarantee bond.
- In both October 1987 and December 1987 he failed to show up for concerts at Louisville Gardens in Louisville, Kentucky. (Sixth and Muhammad Ali Blvd.)

GEORGE "DOES SHOW" JONES

One place he does occasionally show up is Possum Holler Ballroom and Club in "Jones Country," a resort some sixty miles north of Beaumont, Texas. He owns the place.

☆ **Getting There:** Jones Country is in Colesmesneil, Texas. From Beaumont take US 69 north to Colesmesneil. Jones Country is on the main highway, just north of town.

THE LAKE YOU WON'T FIND ON THE MAP

Lake Chargoggagoggmanchauggagoggchaubunagungamaugg near Webster, Massachusetts, is not on any standard issue map and you can see why. There wouldn't be room for any other towns. It has forty-five letters in its name (so you don't have to count.) It is an Indian name that is short for something a lot longer.

☆ **Getting There:** My atlas shortens the name to Lake Chaubunagungamaug. Only seventeen letters. So why don't they shorten Williamsport, Pennsylvania, to Billport? Take Exit 2 east off I-395.

GUNS OR BUTTER

If you live in New York, or have lived in New York, you know the sacrifice you make in housing: small, cramped, expensive, all for the convenience of living in Manhattan. People in other parts of the country don't understand. They think *house* means as large as you can afford. They sacrifice in other areas. But the folks in the mountains of Kentucky and West Virginia understand. They make the same sort of sacrifice. That's why you see so many trailers with satellite dish antennas outside. That's the sacrifice they make for the convenience of hundreds of TV channels.

☆ **Getting There:** On your way to Oak Hill, West Virginia, to see where Hank Williams, Sr., died (see Wipeouts, page 206), take Exit 60 east from I-64-77. It winds around and you'll see numerous trailers with dishes outside.

ALL THIS AND TIFFANY TOO?

Remember when cities had downtowns? Downtowns were killed by malls, those antiseptic suburban monuments to programmed shopping. And not only did the malls kill the downtowns, they gave birth to Tiffany, a peppy teen singer who jump-started her career by singing in mall courts.

The nation's largest mall is the Del Amo Fashion Center in Torrance, California, with three million square feet of space.

How much is three million square feet?

Say Tiffany is five feet tall. And maybe a foot and a half wide. It would take 40,000 Tiffanys stretched end-to-end to make three million square feet.

☆ **Getting There:** It's at 3 Del Amo Fashion Square, and isn't that an imaginative address? From the San Diego

Freeway (I-405) take Carson St. west to Torrance. It's easy to spot.

WHERE MUHAMMAD ALI THREW HIS OLYMPIC GOLD MEDAL INTO THE OHIO RIVER

He was a reigning Olympic boxing champion, a rising star in the fight game, and a proud young black man. But when he tried to eat at a downtown restaurant in Louisville, Kentucky, in the fall of 1960, he was turned away because of his color. Cassius Clay, who would later change his name to Muhammad Ali, was crushed. He had represented his country in the Olympics, but he wasn't even allowed to eat at a respectable restaurant in his hometown.

To add injury to insult he was then chased by a gang of racist bikers. After he and a friend whipped up on the Harley gang, he marched out on the Second Street bridge and without hesitation ripped his Olympic gold medal off and heaved it into the darkness of the Ohio River.

He described his feelings in his autobiography, *The Greatest:* "The Olympic medal had been the most precious thing that had ever come to me. I worshiped it. It was proof of performance, status, a symbol of belonging, of being part of a team, a country, a world. . . . The medal was gone, but the sickness was gone, too. I felt calm, relaxed, confident. . . . I felt a new, secret strength."

☆ **Getting There:** He threw his medal from the middle of the Second St. Bridge. From downtown Louisville take Second St. north to the Ohio River. If you want to park and walk out, there are plenty of metered spaces on Main St.

ORGANIZED SCANDAL TOURS

Baby Boomers, who grew up seeing the sights from the inside of a station wagon, have created their own kind of organized tours: sight-seeing excursions that take them past the homes from the headlines, where famous people murdered and were murdered, where loyal secretaries shredded incriminating documents for their military-haired bosses, where SCANDALS!—yes, I can say it —SCANDALS! occurred.

Here are three of this new breed of sight-seeing tours.

GRAVE LINE TOURS

A macabre tour bus service. Where else but Hollywood?

Grave Line Tours, and its flagship the S.S. Sharon Tate, a gray and black hearse, transports tourists to all the real sights tourists want to visit: the murder sites and final residences of Hollywood stars.

- The hotel on Hollywood Boulevard where female impersonator-actor Divine expired. "He had the courtesy to die on our route," says the tour guide.

- The spot on Hollywood Boulevard where "Fred Mertz hit the Walk of Fame with a thud." (Actor William Frawley collapsed with a fatal heart attack on the walk.)
- The apartment building where actor Jack Cassidy died in a fire. "His family decided to go ahead and have him cremated," says the tour guide. "I understand they got 50 percent off."
- The liquor store where John Belushi threw a temper tantrum shortly before his drug overdose.
- The telephone pole that Montgomery Clift crashed his car into. "We're pretty sure it was this one right here," says the guide. "He broke so many bones in his face he never looked the same again."
- And the most celebrated house on the tour: the mansion where Sharon Tate and her friends met Charles Manson and his friends.

The tour costs $30 per person, lasts about two hours, and takes in about seventy-five sights, from Hollywood to Beverly Hills to Bel Air. And you get a map of southern California cemeteries showing where celebrities are buried. "So you can get within six feet of your favorite star," says the tour guide.

☆ **Getting There:** The Grave Line Tours information number is (213) 876-0920. For reservations call (213) 876-4286. The tour bus leaves daily at noon from the east wall at Grauman's Chinese Theatre (now Mann's Chinese Theatre) at 6925 Hollywood Blvd. From the Hollywood Freeway take Hollywood Blvd. west.

SCANDALS IN THE NATION'S CAPITAL

Washington's Scandal Tours is more slapstick than the Hollywood or New York scandal tours. It is played for laughs, right down to the tour guide, who is a George Bush look-alike.

As the bus passes the White House a Marilyn Monroe impersonator croons a love song to John F. Kennedy. At the Pentagon a phony Fawn Hall sobs that her ex-boss Colonel Oliver North was "the most patriotic man in the universe" as she passes out plastic bags filled with shredded paper and signed "Love, Fawn."

Famous scandal sites on the seventy-five minute tour include the congressional cloak room where, the tour guide says, a homosexual congressman "let his fingers do the walking through the House and Senate pages."

The bus stops behind the Capitol Hill town house where Democratic presidential hopeful Gary Hart was caught entertaining model Donna Rice, and the tour guide shouts, "Everybody out for some fresh air and fresh smut. You're going to get out of the bus, you're going to see it, you're going to touch it, you'll be there."

☆ **Getting There:** The Scandal Tours leave from the Washington Hilton Hotel at 1919 Connecticut Ave. NW. It operates on weekends only. The price is $24. For times of departure call (202) 387-2253.

NEW YORK'S FAMOUS MURDER SITES TOUR

What Grave Line Tours does in Los Angeles and Scandal Tours does in Washington, D.C., Sidewalks of New York Tours does in the Big Apple: shows you where the rich and famous croaked.

Sidewalks' "Famous Murder Sites Tour" walks you past two dozen of New York's many famous fatalities including:

- The former barbershop where gangster Albert Anastasia was blown away by a hit team led by "Crazy Joe" Gallo. "It was a flamboyant killing to show great respect for Albert Anastasia," the tour guide tells you, adding that the barber chair later sold for $7,000.
- Columbus Circle, where mobster Joe Colombo was gunned down in 1971 at an Italian-American unity

rally by a hit man posing as a photographer. Colombo survived, in a coma, until 1978.

- The Osborne, 205 West 57th St., where actor Gig Young killed his wife of three weeks and then himself.

- The sidewalk on West 57th where comedian Fred Allen died while walking his dog.

- The "Broadway Butterfly" murder site where "Broadway Butterfly" Dot King was suffocated with a pillow in the twenties.

- The Metropolitan Opera House, where violinist Helen Hagnes Mintiks was killed by a stagehand during a performance. Her body was found in an air-conditioning shaft.

- The *Looking for Mr. Goodbar* murder site: 253 West 72nd St., where on January 1, 1978, schoolteacher Katherine Cleary was strangled by a man she picked up in a bar.

- The climax of the tour is the site of the Preppie Murder: an elm tree in Central Park where in 1986 eighteen-year-old Jennifer Levin was killed by twenty-year-old Robert Chambers during what he claimed was a bout of "rough sex."

Tour operator Sam Stafford, a former Dallas travel agency owner, says the reason for the success of murder sites tours such as his and the one in LA is simple: "Reading about it in the newspaper is one thing, but standing on the spot is different."

☆ **Getting There:** The cost of the tour is $10. For more information, call (212) 517-0201.

Sidewalks of New York offers fifteen different tours in Manhattan, including:

- "Leona Takes Manhattan" takes you past the apartment building where Harry Helmsley met wife-to-be Leona; the restaurant where he proposed to her; the stores where Leona bought personal items that she billed to the hotel company.

- "A Tour Named Jackie," includes visits to former first lady Jackie Kennedy Onassis's drugstore, the resale shop where she sells her old clothing, and her favorite florist.
- "Beverly Hills East" is a guide to the Manhattan homes of movie stars.

FOR FURTHER READING

Here is my recommended reading list for unauthorized travelers.

NEWSPAPERS AND MAGAZINES

USA Today is the best source for coverage of celebrity arrests and trials, mass-media murders, and legitimate UFO and Bigfoot sightings.

The *National Enquirer* covers celebrities like the *New York Times* covers the world—seriously.

Weekly World News, a weekly tabloid, is your best source for two-headed baby stories. They broke the Elvis Lives story.

People magazine doesn't always give the addresses but they are the best at getting celebrities to tell their side of the story. And pose at the scene of the crime.

Spy magazine has a regular Spy Map, which is usually a guide to unauthorized spots in Manhattan (where future assassins stayed was in one issue). It also has an occasional Spy Trip to a very strange place.

Memories is a bimonthly filled with nostalgia. It usually relives a famous crime or scandal in each issue.

Rolling Stone doesn't weigh in on scandal very often but when it does, the articles are detailed, thorough, and include lots of addresses.

For more mob sites, the April 1989 issue of *Chicago* magazine has an excellent list.

BOOKS

Any unauthorized celebrity biography and the thicker the better.

Hollywood Babylon by Kenneth Anger (Straight Arrow, 1975)—Down-and-dirty gossip mongering from a Hollywood insider. This is the original unauthorized travel guide, even if it doesn't always list addresses or directions.

Hollywood Babylon II by Kenneth Anger (Plume, 1984) —The sequel! Worth it just for the cover photo of Liz Taylor during her porker period.

Nashville Babylon by Randall Riese (Congdon & Weed, 1988)—Does for Country Music USA what Anger did for Tinseltown.

This Is Hollywood by Ken Schlesser (Universal Books, 1988)—The best shirt pocket guide to Hollywood scandal sites.

The Movie Lover's Guide to Hollywood by Richard Alleman (Harper & Row, 1985)—The scandal sites are here, but this book goes beyond scandal to legitimate movie sights.

The Movie Lover's Guide to New York by Richard Alleman (Harper & Row, 1988)—An East Coast version.

Fallen Angels: Chronicles of L.A. Crime and Mystery by Marvin J. Wolf and Katherine Mader (Ballantine, 1986) —A thorough guide to murder and mayhem in El Lay. It includes directions.

America Off the Wall/The West Coast by Kristan Lawson and Anneli S. Rufus (Wiley, 1989)—Tends toward the weird, but that's okay, too.

Amazing America by Jane and Michael Stern (Random House, 1978)—Also focuses on the weird.

GEOGRAPHICAL INDEX OF SITES

THE SOUTH

Alabama

Arkansas

Florida

THE WEST

INDEX OF NAMES

—

INDEX OF SITES AND SUBJECTS